Transforming your ANGER in non-violent ways

Peter Burton

Speechmark

Transforming your ANGER in non-violent ways

Peter Burton

Speechmark

Published by
Speechmark Publishing Ltd, 70 Alston Drive, Bradwell Abbey, Milton Keynes
MK13 9HG, United Kingdom
Tel: +44 (0) 1908 326944 Fax: +44 (0) 1908 326960
www.speechmark.net

002-5616/Printed in the United Kingdom by CMP (uk) Limited

British Library Cataloguing in Publication Data
A catalogue record for this book is available from the British Library.

ISBN 978 0 86388 754 3

FSC MIX Paper FSC® C004309

Contents

Introduction

I once got so exasperated with my son Ross that I punched a hole in our landing wall. He was five years old at the time. At this moment, I felt like I was five too. He looked at me. He looked at the wall. Then a little grin came over his face as if to say: 'What are you going to do now, dad?'

That evening, sitting down over a cup of tea, I thought to myself: 'There has to be a different way, a better way to deal with my irritation, exasperation and anger than bashing a hole in a wall.'

I really didn't want to be communicating with my five-year-old, my other sons, the youngsters I was teaching at the time, or indeed anybody, in the way I did that day when I was feeling that way. So I made a commitment to find other and better ways to communicate when I was feeling angry.

I can only guess that you are reading this book because you, or someone you care about, are having some problems related to anger.

The purpose of this book is not to help you manage your anger, nor to control it or deal with it. My aim is to introduce you to some methods that I have found helpful in fully and safely expressing anger since 'the wall experience' described above. I'm doing this so that you can transform your anger into something that is of real and lasting value.

So what does transforming anger non-violently mean?

I first encountered the expression 'non-violent' when, one day in 1997, a friend of mine I was working with at the time said: 'Hey, there's a one-day class in London being led by an American called Marshall Rosenberg. He teaches something called "non-violent communication". I think it'll be really interesting. Shall we go?' The class cost £50. It has been one of the most important investments of my adult life. Marshall Rosenberg, in his book *Non-violent Communication: A Language of Compassion* (Rosenberg, 1999), suggests that the violence that we as humans experience is not so much the image of physical violence that we might imagine when we hear the word, but rather the violence that comes from very well-formed thoughts and spoken words, those such as 'should', 'ought', 'have to', must' and 'got to'.

These are words that tell us we have no choice, no freedom: that we are on the receiving end of another's power. And if we do not do the things that we have to do, or are supposed to do, then we are either labelling ourselves or being labelled by others with words such as 'lazy', 'disobedient', 'thoughtless', 'inconsiderate', and so on. In other words, we are using words as labels to describe other people, as if we were fixed and unchanging objects displayed in a museum. 'Moralistic judgement' is the adult term for this type of language.

I prefer to think of these 'should' words as members of a very dangerous gang. Why dangerous? Because they hunt in packs, stealthily and 'under the radar'. This makes their detection very difficult.

I call them the 'should gang'.

How we can detect when these dangerous gang members are taking control of our lives and how we can translate their message is one way that I have learned to transform my anger in a non-violent way.

I learned a second way during that same year. For some time I had heard about neuro-linguistic programming (NLP), so after attending a course, I qualified as an NLP practitioner.

The third element I am drawing on is something that I have discovered much more recently. Emotional freedom technique (EFT) is based on the same premise as acupuncture, namely that we have electrical energy flowing through channels or meridians in our body. When the flow of energy gets hindered or blocked as a result of an earlier emotional trauma, we can behave in ways that are reactive, habitual and unhelpful. Phobias of all types, cravings, addictions and situations and people we feel excessively angry about, are some of the emotional responses that have become locked into our minds and bodies, thus removing the freedom of choice, leading to habitual reactions which often create problems for us.

These are the three ingredients that I shall be sharing with you in order to help you transform your anger in a non-violent way. With each of the three, what really makes the difference is a change of mindset and attitude. I have realised that once I embrace a different mindset and attitude, then my actual perception of the world around me alters and, equally importantly, my perception of myself changes too.

This understanding has enabled me to deal with other people and life situations in a better way, and this is what I expect for you too, if you are willing to make use of any of the methods and resources featured here.

Inevitably with any book, there is a limit to the amount I can explain, describe and teach, and only so much you can learn. If any explanations or resources appeal to you, and you find them to be helpful, I would definitely encourage you to pursue them by reading further, as well as attending training courses on the three main domains of knowledge that I have drawn on for this book.

This book is about change. It is about changing the ways in which you have got used to expressing your anger.

I wonder what has kept you from changing?

Ever since I encountered it many years ago, I have liked this saying:
'One definition of insanity is to keep doing the same thing and expect a different outcome.'

When I was learning person-centred counselling back in the early 1990s, I encountered another saying with a similar theme: 'If you always do what you always did, you'll always get what you always got.'

I would like you to be able to use anger as a way to help you connect with what is really going on inside you underneath the anger and, as a result, allow you to make the kind of communication with others that you yearn for.

From my own experience and that of those I have worked with, it seems that when we express anger in the habitual way that most of us have learned to express it then - guess what? - the very thing we yearn for disappears over the horizon in the opposite direction. 'Drat!' we think. 'I am getting exactly the opposite of what I wanted. How did this happen again?'

I know you believe you understand what you think I said, but I am not sure you realise that what you heard is not what I meant.

What I mean is that often we experience misunderstanding that leads to anger. Have you ever had that experience? I wonder if something like this was going on in the following story.

What on earth...?

I saw something the other day that beggared belief. I literally could not believe my eyes. I was driving home and came up to a big motorway junction. It's one of those roundabouts that I know well and often feel uncomfortable driving round, especially at rush hour.

Why? Because it has lanes that shift as you go round them, so that the lane you were in to start with is the wrong lane for your exit by the time you want to exit.

Does this sound familiar to you? Most towns seem to have their own roundabout or junction that, when it is talked about, people roll their eyes and say: 'Oh yes, I know the place you mean!'

Anyway, on this day I'm describing, I see ahead of me a seven-seater car indicating to come into the nearside lane, the driver realising that they were in the wrong lane for their exit. The car pulled into the lane in front of a regular saloon car. What happened then, and for the next half mile, was quite extraordinary.

The driver in the saloon car responded by flashing his lights and sounding his horn. 'They sound pretty displeased,' I thought.

Then the saloon accelerated, overtook the seven-seater and braked sharply, forcing it to do likewise. The seven-seater then overtook the saloon and I can only find this expression to attempt to sum up what was going on in both drivers: 'Game on!'

For the next half mile or so, I witnessed both cars flashing lights, honking horns, overtaking followed by sharp braking, pulling alongside and steering towards the other car, forcing it dangerously close to the kerb.

Both these drivers had clearly 'lost the plot'. What I found really scary to realise was that neither driver seemed to have any thought, awareness or regard, not only for their own safety, but for the safety of other drivers, passengers and cars around them.

Eventually, after about a half a mile, just after a roundabout, both cars pulled over on the pavement, and all I saw as I drove past (I only mediate between people by invitation!), were two 50-something males whose faces told me that it was unlikely they were going to exchange birthday cards.

'What on earth,' I wondered, 'was going on for each of those drivers that, in the space of seconds, they changed from reasonable people who probably are, or had been, husbands, dads, granddads, neighbours and work colleagues, into some crazed Ben-Hur-style charioteers with little or no regard for their own or others' well-being?'

Now, becoming angry when driving is something that happens to me very rarely, and I do not ever remember experiencing anything like what those two drivers were experiencing on that morning, an experience that could most accurately be described as 'road rage'.

Yet when I told this story to my partner, she told me of a similar incident many years before where she was one of the people involved. One telling phrase she used was: 'I didn't care what happened. It was like a switch went on inside me that meant that I didn't care what happened – even to die would have been OK.' Wow! Something very powerful is going on in us, isn't it, if mature adults, male or female, can change like this in a moment?

And then I remembered the 'wall' incident with Ross and another incident when on holiday with my family in France I berated my eldest son Jack over the subject of an apple. But now I'm curious: What was happening to me back then? How come there were moments when I snapped? What was it that led me to lose control, just for a moment?

And, if I lost control for that moment, could I also regain control in a moment? Or, better still, head my anger off, 'ambush' it and transform it, before I did something that I would deeply regret?

And, when I started to remember past events more carefully, what I got very curious about was how there were other times, when my sons, other family members, friends and work colleagues were doing or saying virtually the same things, but I reacted very differently, without anger.

My curiosity

That is the curiosity that has led me to investigate this thing called 'anger' and what has led me to write here about what it is, how it affects us and how we can transform it in ways that are anything but violent.

So what is anger?

What I have learned is that anger is a constantly changing maelstrom.

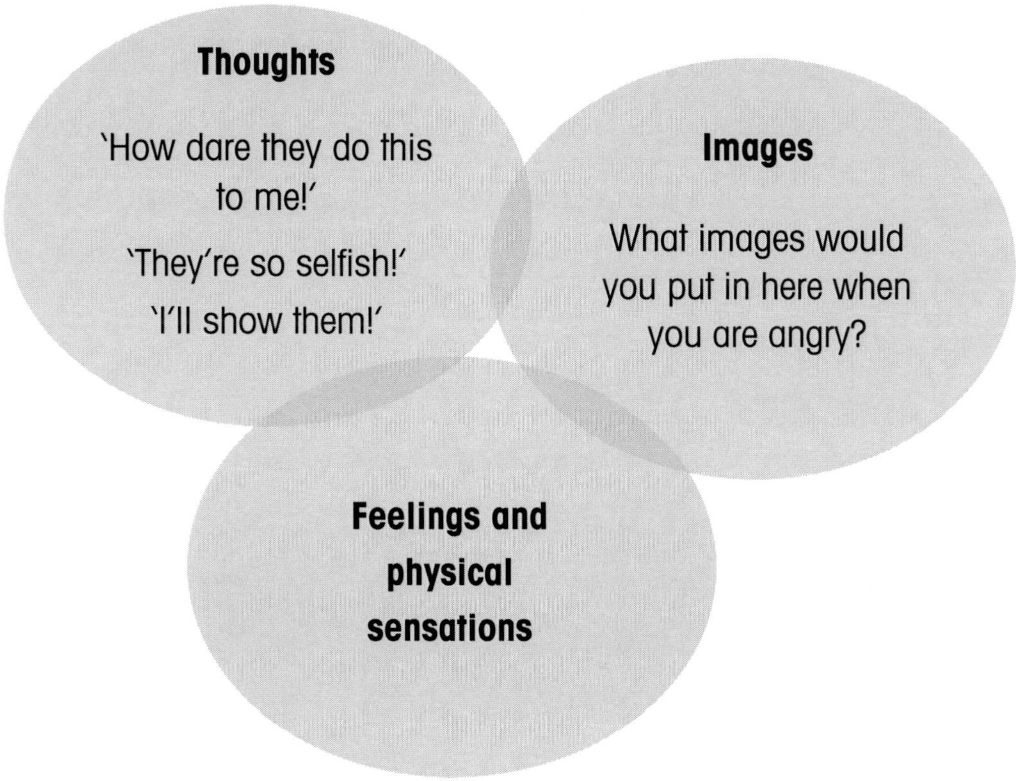

The make-up of anger

As I said earlier, this is not a book about managing, controlling or dealing with anger. To me, these expressions can suggest that anger needs to be suppressed, which I believe is part of an overall problem.

No, this is a book designed to help you express your anger fully and safely by going below the surface and transforming it into what is really going on inside you.

Now, although I love popular music, it reinforces the common yet mistaken belief that the other people are not only the stimulus, but also the cause of my feelings. Whether you are remembering Carole King's 'You Make Me Feel Like A Natural Woman', or Sylvester's 'You Make Me Feel Mighty Real' (what feeling is that exactly? Not to worry; I still like the music!), the popular notion is the same, namely that 'you make me feel'.

What lies at the heart of this book is my suggestion to you that anger is an 'inside job', which is not caused by anyone or anything that is 'out there'.

So the bad news is that we are the cause of our anger.
And the good news?

We are the cause of our anger!

Why is that good news? Because we can change our habits, even when they are habits of a lifetime, if the motivation is strong enough. And one of the habits that I have found helpful to develop is to start thinking and saying, 'I am feeling angry because I am telling myself x', and then noticing what the actual thoughts are that going on inside my head. Previously I would think and say: 'I am feeling angry because you did this or said that.'

This may seem a small point and in some ways it is. But just as a mosquito is a very small insect, if you have ever shared a sleeping bag with one you will know that the effects can be dramatic. So, too, have I found the seemingly small turnaround of that sentence above quite dramatic, in a far more beneficial way than being bitten by a mosquito.

I realise now that I was not expressing my anger fully and safely at all by hitting that wall or shouting at my class. Nor were the two drivers who threatened the safety of themselves and so many others on that very ordinary morning.

They and I were confusing the stimulus with the cause of anger in a way that I believe is very common. The consequence of this confusion stopped me engaging with my anger fully, stopped me diving under the surface to find what my anger was really about, and then missing the chance to grasp and use the pearl of personal truth and wisdom that lay at the heart of me.

I've no idea what the outcome was of the altercation between the two drivers, but I am confident that if they knew what I'm going to share with you in this book, they would have had a much more peaceful and easy ride to their destination, as would all of the other drivers around them.

What is this thing called anger?

There are differing schools of thought about anger and its origins. You may find it helpful to have three of them described. Each accepts that feelings, thoughts and behaviours are key elements, but each places a different emphasis on each element. I find that this is helpful up to a point but, as I shall explain shortly, they each lack a key component.

What that key component is and how to pin it down and share it with others is a core element of this book.

A behaviourist approach

As their name suggests, behaviourists believe that people's behaviour is the main thing on which to focus attention. They suggest that how we have learned to behave is the result of past rewards and punishments.

For example, if I have shouted at somebody with a certain kind of tone to my voice and a certain kind of look on my face in order to get that somebody to do what I want, and it works, then the 'reward' means that I'm very likely to use the same approach in the future. A consequence of this, however, may be that I become a 'one-trick pony', getting stuck on using one approach, regardless of the situation and from whom I want something.

So, if I used the same approach with a different person in a different situation, and the response was a punishing one, behaviourists suggest that I would be less likely to repeat the behaviour in future, because my learning would be 'the behaviour I've just used does not get me what I want'.

This approach is shown diagrammatically below.

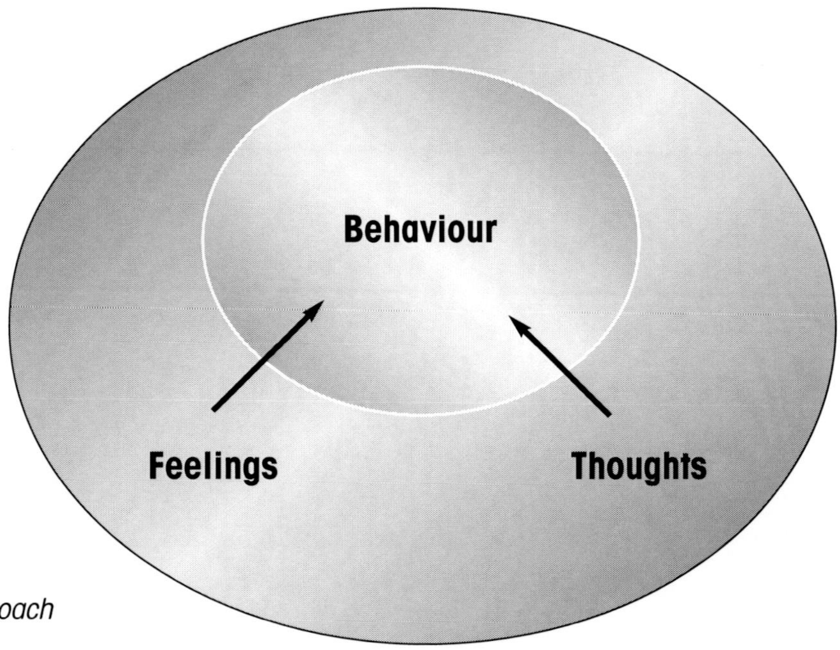

A behaviourist approach

A psychodynamic approach

This approach, the modern architect of which is Sigmund Freud, placed feelings as the main driver of our behaviour. When we sense certain feelings and impulses surfacing which we would rather did not surface, we behave in ways that are designed to prevent them arising. Freud described these behaviours as 'defence mechanisms'.

So with anger, for example, he described 'displacement' as a typical behaviour arising from feelings or impulses that would be very unlikely to be acted on: indeed, to even imagine acting on them is likely to create much anxiety and stress.

What sort of thing do I mean? Imagine a parent becoming angry with a child over something like being late for school. What the child might feel as a result of being on the receiving end of the parent's anger is anger at the parent, and maybe the impulse to want to hurt the parent. This combination of feeling and impulse may provoke much anxiety in the child because there will be many contrary thoughts, feelings and images that tell the child: 'This response is not a safe one and could lead to greater harm than I'm experiencing at the moment. Better to "button my lip" and just take it.'

However, the feeling and impulse don't go away. They seek to be satisfied. So along comes younger brother or younger sister or smaller child in the playground or some such person who will be a much safer recipient of the stored feeling and impulse. This takes us into the territory of 'projection' and 'transference', which are beyond the scope of this book, but I have found them to be fascinating subjects in their own right in helping to explain what our motivations are for doing what we do. These motivations can sometimes baffle us until we achieve a different perspective about what's happening 'below the surface' of us.

The figure below represents this approach.

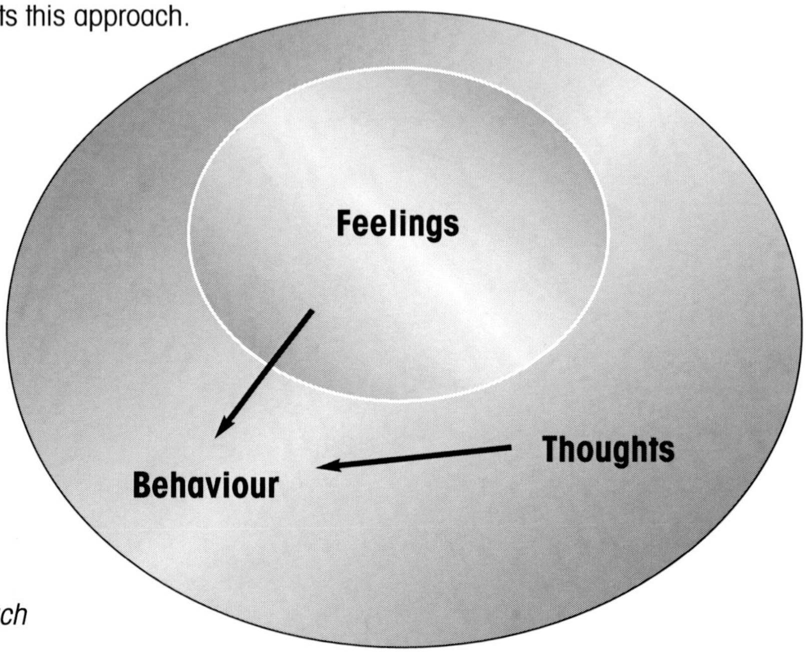

A psychodynamic approach

A cognitive-behavioural approach

This third approach puts our thinking at the helm of our behaviour.

A cognitive-behavioural approach says that it's our thinking in response to something that happens to us which affects or even creates our feelings, which in turn influence, create or drive our behaviour.
In the case of Nelson Mandela, for example, I find it easy to imagine feelings of anger and thoughts of revenge simmering away for the years he was incarcerated, just waiting to be let go when he was released. But clearly this was not what happened or, if it did to start with, those feelings and thoughts changed significantly during his prison sentence.

Likewise, I remember reading of a passenger on the London Underground who described his irritation at the behaviour of a father he described as 'irresponsible' and his 'unruly' children. The man could finally stand it no longer, and asked if the father could do something to control his children. The father replied: 'None of us knows what to do. We've just come from our last visit to the hospital where my wife and their mother is just about to die.'

The passenger described his feelings moving from anger and irritation to compassion and consideration in a split second, purely as a result of the change in what he was thinking and how he was judging the father and children.

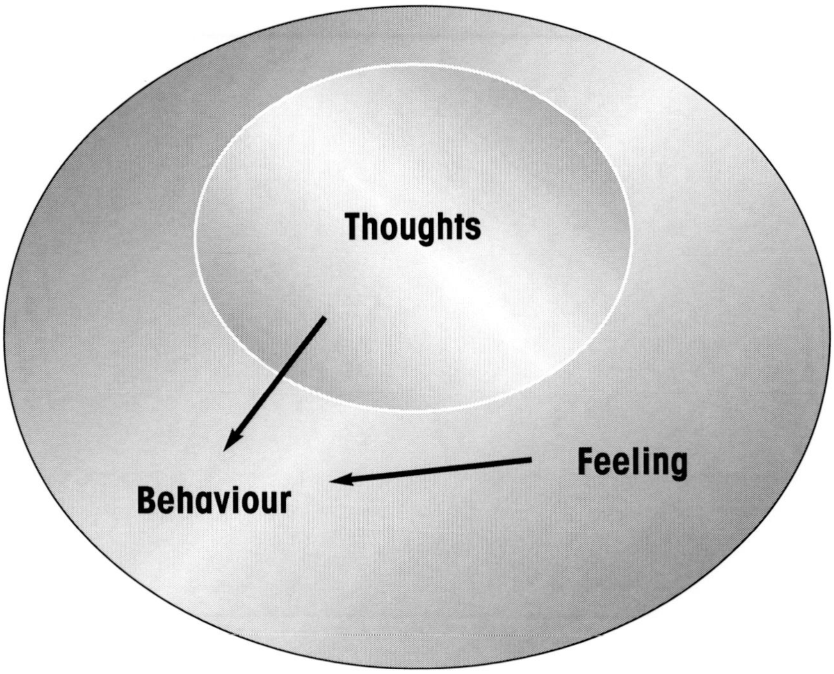

A cognitive-behavioural approach

Shakespeare as therapist

So, the cognitive-behavioural view is that nothing external makes us angry – it's our thinking in relation to something that someone has done or said that creates the anger.

There seem to be two types of pain that we experience:

- physical pain
- emotional pain.

Where problems can occur for us is when we muddle up the origins of our pain and our response, treating these two types of pain as if they were one and the same.

Say a wasp stung you. That sting causes you pain, yes?

And if we lined up a hundred people, and got a wasp to sting each person (this is just an imaginary experiment, OK?), then to a lesser or greater extent, each person would feel physical pain caused by the sting.

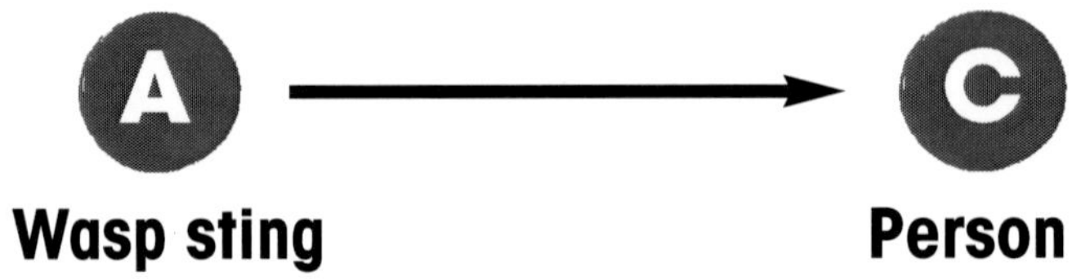

The effect of a wasp sting

Now, however, with the same hundred people, imagine each person being called an insulting name. Does each person feel the same way now?

I am suggesting that some would feel hurt, some would feel angry, some would be mildly amused, and some would just shrug it off.

Why does each person not feel the same as if a wasp stung them? What is the difference between these two events?

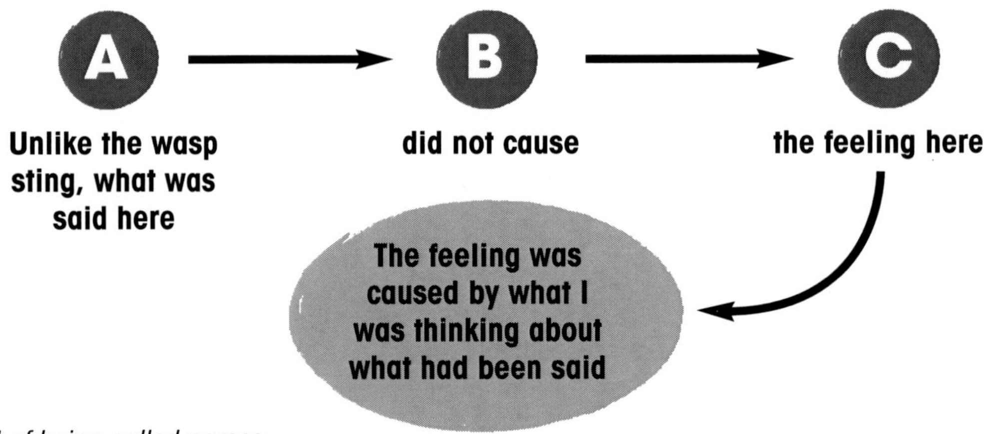

The effect of being called names

Although we wouldn't normally think of him in these terms, perhaps Shakespeare was an early advocate of this when he has the character of Hamlet saying, 'There is nothing good nor bad but thinking makes it so.'

A more modern variation on this theme of perception is probably familiar to you. It's to do with a glass filled halfway up with water.

If I asked you to imagine such a glass on a table in front of you, would you say that it was half full or half empty?

I have never conducted a survey of people myself in regard to this question, but what I tell myself is that there would be some people who would give one response and some who would give the other.

Obvious? I hope so.

So what?

Just before we move on, let me share a brief story with you, which I like and use to illustrate this point.

The petrol station

A customer called into a petrol station and went in to pay. There were two assistants working there that day and the customer said to the one serving, 'What's this town like? I'm thinking of moving from where I am.'

The assistant asked, 'What's it like where you live now?'

'Oh,' said the customer, 'it's horrible. I don't feel safe there, my neighbours don't speak to me, my work is dull and time just drags.'

'Well,' the assistant replied, 'I'm afraid it's pretty much like that round here too. I'm not sure that you'd like it so much.'

A little while later, another customer drove in, filled up and came inside to pay. They were served by the same assistant, and asked, 'What's it like around here, only I'm thinking of moving from where I live at the moment?'

Again the assistant asked, 'What's it like where you live right now?'

'Oh,' said the customer, 'I shall be so sad to leave. I feel safe there, my neighbours are really friendly and it's only because I have the chance of being promoted in my work, which I really enjoy, that means I'm thinking of moving.'

'Well,' said the assistant, 'I'm glad to say it's just like that round here, and if you do move, I'm sure you'll soon be enjoying it as much as where you are now.'

When the customer left, the assistant's colleague turned and said, 'I don't get it. Those customers asked you the same question, yet you gave different answers. Which was true?'

What would you say? Was the customer's 'glass' half full or half empty?

Anger is an inside job

What this simple example of the glass and the story both say to me forms a key premise of this book, namely that our perceptions and our beliefs, which are internally created, are powerfully linked. As a result of this linkage, the consequences are powerful and significant. So powerful and significant, in fact, that it perhaps explains the growing interest, shown by the films *The Secret* (2006) and *What the Bleep?* (2006) in what is known as 'the law of attraction'.

What does this 'law' say? It's a fuller version of the Shakespeare quote and the glass of water examples above, and has echoes of the Henry Ford quote: 'Whether you think you can, or think you can't, you're right.'

What this 'law' suggests is that what we pay regular attention to with our thoughts and feelings not only affects our behaviour but also can actually attract the very things, people and situations that we want or do not want in our lives.

This includes the anger that shows up in ourselves and in those around us.

When I first heard about this, I remember thinking, 'Well, I understand about attracting the things I want, but I'm confused about getting things I don't want. How does this work?' Let me give you an example of how I make sense of it.

I'm going to ask you to stop thinking about the shape below by closing your eyes and putting it out of your mind. Ready? OK, please do not think about the triangle with the word 'blue' inside it. Now close your eyes or cover the shape up and put it out of your mind.

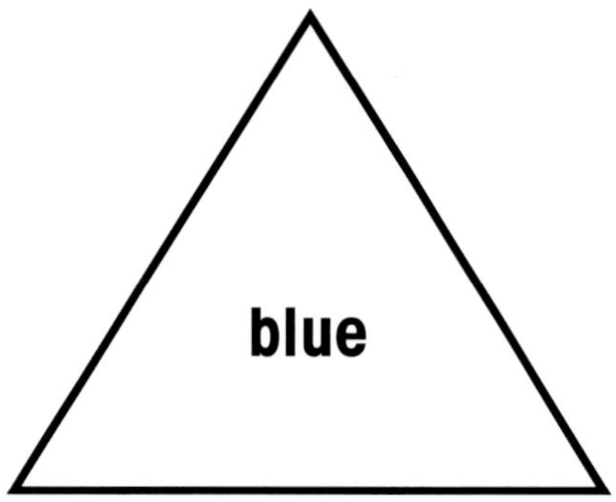

What has just happened?
If you are like most people I have done this with, you will have seen in your mind's eye a triangle with the word 'blue' inside it, or can still see it somewhere in your mind despite making your best effort not to. This may help you to understand more about the way that your brain processes information and makes sense of the world around you. It seems that human brains are able only to comprehend that which is stated in the positive.

With my example of the triangle, it seems that the brain first has to 'see' the shape before it can attempt to 'not see' it. Is this making sense to you?

And if you are thinking, 'Well, it was because that shape was actually drawn on a page, so I could actually see it', you might want to close your eyes and aim to 'not see' a circle with the word 'red' inside it, or any other shape and colour of your choice, and then notice what difference there is for you, if any. With any statement that features 'don't want', or indeed, any negative instruction, it will come as no surprise if we do the very thing that we do not want to do!

This has particular resonance for parents, teachers and those adults living and working with children and young people. Do you hear yourself telling them not to run across the road, not to speak to you like that, not to treat their brother or sister or classmate or fellow young people with disrespect?

And can you now hear what message they are actually receiving?

- 'Run across the road.'
- 'Speak to me like that.'
- 'Treat others with disrespect.'

The focus of this book

The focus of this book is not to challenge existing theories, but rather to explain and describe what I mean by using 'non-violent ways' of transforming anger. In particular, many of the examples and exercises come from three different bodies of knowledge that I have studied and make use of in my own life.

These three are:

- non-violent communication (NVC)
- neuro-linguistic programming (NLP)
- emotional freedom technique (EFT).

All of my learning and what I see happening around me supports my basic premise that anger is an 'inside job', which of course means that the way to transform it also lives inside us.

What I mean by this is that anger is created within us by the meaning we make and by our response to what has happened outside of us. With the methods that I've learned, and the experiences that I've had (both positive and not so positive with regard to anger), I have come to the conclusion that the three approaches discussed at the start of this chapter as ways to understand our behaviour are useful, but one key element is missing. I believe this element to be vital, not only to our understanding of anger and its transformation, but for understanding what sits at the core of us.

The three bodies of knowledge I have highlighted above all include this 'missing ingredient', which is why I have found them to be of so much use.

I agree that there are thoughts, feelings and behaviours active in us constantly, but a key question for me is: 'To what end? What purpose do they serve?'

For me, the answer is simple, and the effect profound.

We humans are needs-driven creatures, therefore all of our behaviours are ways, or strategies, to get our needs met. And our thoughts and our feelings help us to work out whether our needs are being met or not met at any one given moment.

In a nutshell, if we are experiencing thoughts that are judgemental, coming from the 'should gang', then they will almost inevitably be creating feelings that are unpleasant, and it's highly likely that our needs are not being met. And if our thoughts are kindly, generous or indeed absent, then our feelings are highly likely to be ones we enjoy, which means that our needs are being met.

This allows us to take the very important next step, that of making a request, which I shall explain in more detail later in this chapter as it forms one part of a simple-to-learn five-step formula, which I have learned and teach others to use in order to get their needs met in a peaceable way.

It has been my experience that making a request is relatively straightforward. What was harder for me in the early days, and has been for those I've worked with subsequently, is being able to identify and to name what those feelings and needs actually are.

It has not been my experience to come across many adults who have been very well-trained, schooled or brought up to work out what they are needing.

The habit that we seem to have developed much more fully is to create and share certain kinds of thoughts, those that we call opinions and judgements.

What I am drawing on here is that body of knowledge called 'non-violent communication', a method that has been developed by Dr Marshall Rosenberg, and which I have been learning and applying since I encountered it back in 1997 at that one-day workshop in London.

Its relevance to anger is clear to me, for there seem to be at least three things happening to us when we experience anger:

- We are often feeling something else that the anger is masking, for example, upset.
- We are likely to be blaming someone or something else for not getting what we need.
- We are about to speak or act in such a way that will almost guarantee that we will not get what we need, and may even come to regret.

So I'm back to the suggestion that when we are angry, we are often focusing almost exclusively on what we do not want. We behave in a way that is likely to give us the very opposite of what we actually need, and pay attention to our thoughts about the wrongness and badness of the others who are involved, rather than on what we actually need.

Typically, there are three thoughts that fuel our anger and keep us stuck, like the younger monk in the story below.

- Thought 1: how right, virtuous and good a person I am.
- Thought 2: how nasty, bad, evil and vindictive the other person is.
- Thought 3: once they agree with me, come round to my way of thinking and behave in a way that I want them to, then all will be well.

Guess what the other person or people involved in an angry exchange are thinking?

Correct! Exactly the same.

So, in my experience, these specific thoughts will perpetuate anger for as long as we are alive. I do not subscribe to the view that time is a healer. I am convinced that we take our unresolved anger to our deathbed.

This story illustrates this point well.

The two monks

There were two monks making the long walk back to their monastery, when they came to a river recently swollen by heavy rain. A woman, clearly in some distress, stood by the river bank, looking longingly at the other side.

The monks were from an order that forbade any conversation and contact with women, so imagine the surprise of the younger monk when his older companion walked up to the woman, asked her a question, listened to her answer, and to the younger monk's horror, picked her up, carried her across the river and set her down carefully on the opposite bank.

The two monks continued their journey in silence until they came in sight of the monastery. The younger monk could keep silent no longer and hissed, 'How could you do that? How could you break our solemn vow not to make contact with women?'

The older monk turned, looked his fellow in the eye and said, 'Brother, why are you still carrying her? I let her go as soon as I put her down on the river bank.'

This story also has echoes of a saying I like that comes from Confucius:
'Before embarking on a journey of revenge, dig two graves.'

And another phrase that I use but do not know its origin of comes to mind, again about revenge:
'Revenge is like drinking poison, hoping the other will die.'

I extend this to include not only anger and revenge, but also grudges and resentment, which seem to me to be like acid corroding our very system and the quality of the relationships that we have with others.

So although it may sound too simple or fanciful to suggest that focusing on our thoughts, feelings and needs will transform our own or someone else's anger, that has been my personal experience and that of those I have taught or worked with directly.

Perhaps like you, I have also had many experiences where I behaved exactly as I was educated and brought up to do, paying close attention to and behaving in ways that come from thinking one or more of those three thoughts.

I know which I prefer.

So anger can be experienced as an emotional messenger, serving an important purpose whose message is twofold:

1 Something is not OK in my world.
2 Here's some energy to do something about it.

The weakness of anger, however, is that it gives you no further direction or instruction. If you bought a tin marked 'Anger', there would be no instructions for its use, and when you opened the lid, you could be opening a can of worms, a volcano, a pressure cooker or a big bottle of fizzy drink that's just been shaken violently.

So anger is an important messenger, but a poor guide. And if you are not careful, you end up trusting the guide, following it along a well-worn path and realising it has taken you into a cul-de-sac – again! What this means in reality is that you have developed a single style of expressing anger, which has become fixed and habitual. So even if it does not work well for us, or there are many other consequences that we do not enjoy, we still persist because it is what we know. We are, after all, creatures of habit. As the saying goes, 'If the only tool you have is a hammer, then every problem looks like a nail.'

The legendary family therapist 'Virginia Satir' and Richard Bandler, the co-founder of NLP, were in conversation after he had witnessed a session she had led (Bandler, 2008).
She quizzed him. 'What is the strongest instinct that people have, Richard?'
He came back with the reply that he had always given: 'Survival.'
'Not so,' she replied. 'In my experience it is fear of loss of the known and familiar that drives people to keep things as they are and do all they can to resist change.'

How true is this for you, I wonder?

If this rings at all true for you, you may want to look at 'The rubber band of change' (number 37) exercise in the resources section of the book.

One activity that I use regularly with others, employs the image of an onion to explain how anger is an 'inside job.'

It is the best example I have yet come across and constantly has people rethinking their understanding of where their anger stems from.

1 I was feeling angry because I was telling myself 'x'.

2 As well as anger, what I was also feeling was 'x'.

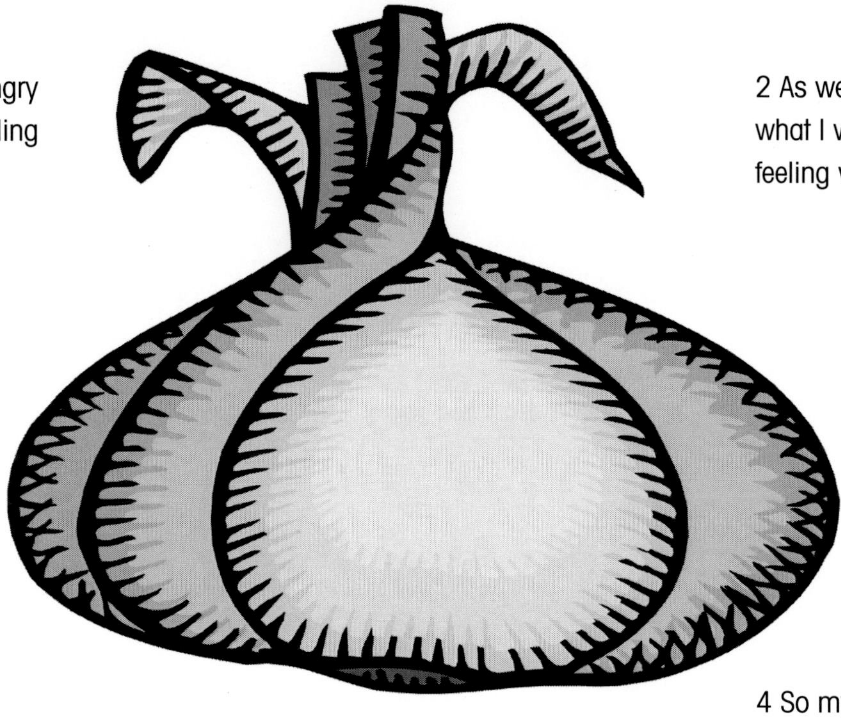

3 What I needed but was not getting was 'x'.

4 So my request to myself or the other person is 'x'.

The anger onion

So as an activity you can do yourself, it goes like this:

1 Take a piece of plain paper.
2 Fold it in half.
3 Draw the shape of an onion as above.
4 Remember a time when you felt angry with yourself, someone else or a situation.
5 Unfold your paper.
6 Write out the first of the four statements below the drawing of your onion and complete it in your own words.
7 Do the same for each of the remaining three statements.

The notorious 'should gang'

Notice whether in statement 1 there are any words in your completed sentence that belong to the 'should gang'. This notorious gang has such 'members' in it as the 'shoulds', the 'oughts', the 'have tos', the 'got tos', the 'musts', the 'cannots' and the 'will nots'.

To give them their grammatical name, they are the 'moral imperative' gang and, to me, they represent the violence that is alive in us. This is not the sort of violence that we typically imagine, with people physically hurting each other, although anger taken to extremes can show itself in just such a way. What I am suggesting to you is that if we allow this 'gang' to inform how we communicate and relate to ourselves and to each other, then a regular experience of unproductive conflict and anger is inevitable. Why? Because these gang members live by having to be right and seeking to wield power over others in order to get their own way. And their own way comes from a fictional world of perfection, a world and a worldview that tolerates no mistakes.

And if the unthinkable happens, and mistakes are made, then punishment is the automatic response, along with the threat of being cast out of the gang. So the gang needs active members who subscribe to its rules in order to thrive, just as a living organism needs nourishment to grow and spread.

I spent a large part of my life being led by this gang's leaders and being a fully signed-up member. Since 1997, however, I have discovered a different way to go about life, a different way of treating myself and a different way of relating to others.

The five-step formula

What I am suggesting is that what most of us have learned very well is to create and deliver opinions and moralistic judgements of others and ourselves. An attack from the 'should gang' can seem to be invisible. They strike rapidly and 'under the radar'.

How do you know if they have paid you a visit?

1. Stop.
2. Pay attention to what you are thinking and saying.
3. Are you criticising others or yourself?
4. Are you offering advice and suggestions when they are not asked for?

If you answered 'yes' to 3 and 4, then I am suggesting that you have become disconnected from your very lifeblood, the very essence of what makes you human, namely your feelings and your needs.

One key thing that I have learned to pay attention to in all communication is my intention. And yet, we are so rarely asked to pay this any heed at all.

When was the last time you were asked or asked yourself: 'What is your intention behind speaking at this moment?'

Most families, most schools, most workplaces and the mass media are very influential here, with a habitual focus on:

- problems
- accusation
- blame.

What I prefer and what I feel uplifted by, although I did not find it very easy to begin with, is to pay attention to:

- ownership of a problem
- responsibility for my actions
- accountability to others for the consequences of my actions.

By others, I mean family members, classmates, work colleagues, neighbours and/or fellow members of an interest group.

To be asked what we are feeling and needing may seem relatively unusual questions, and I would say that at the moment, our ability to identify and express our feelings and needs lags a long way behind our ability to deliver an opinion, a judgement or a stinging rebuke and admonition.

If I have done something that someone else has got angry about, and I face the prospect of being on the receiving end of someone's anger delivered in what I will call the 'traditional way', with messages delivered unedited from the 'should gang', then is it any wonder that I am going to deny my involvement or try to justify my actions, or claim that it was only fair because of what the other person did to me yesterday, the day before or last week?

I am highly likely to fear for my safety (emotional, or in some cases, physical), so I will be anything but honest.

So warfare or capitulation are the likely outcomes from such a way of responding to anger, neither of which creates an environment that I wish to be a part of. How about you?

And that is what attracts me to use the formula below. I have adapted this from the non-violent communication domain described earlier.

How to apply the five-step formula

Step 1: What has happened or is happening? (Imagine recording what is happening on a camcorder or microphone.)

Step 2: What are you thinking? (Ask yourself whether it is more helpful to translate this silently into feelings and needs before you say anything.)

Step 3: What am I feeling?

Step 4: What am I needing that I am not getting?

Step 5: What request am I making of others or myself in a do-able form that aims to get my needs met?

A chance to practise

Here are a few examples of situations that have led to people feeling angry. Imagine yourself in the situation and have a go at using the five-step formula.

Situation: I was not allowed to go skating

I was thinking 'x'

I was feeling 'y' because I was needing 'z'

What I'd like is 'w'

Situation: someone said I was cheating in a card game

I was thinking 'x'

I was feeling 'y' because I was needing 'z'

What I'd like is 'w'

Situation: a friend called the top I was wearing 'ugly'

I was thinking 'x'

I was feeling 'y' because I was needing 'z'

What I'd like is 'w'

Can you think of a recent time when you got angry with yourself or someone else?

Write out what happened and how you were affected by it.

Then apply the five-step formula to translating your original description about what happened and how you were affected by it.

Another way to explain the above is shown in the table below.

Which game do you want to play?

The game of giving and receiving	The game of naming and blaming
My aims	*My aims*
To make life great for myself and others	To be right
To meet everyone's needs	To get what I want
To create community and share power with others	To create a hierarchy and have power over others
My motivation	*My motivation*
Joy	Fear
Harmony	Guilt
Peace	Shame
Meeting needs	Obligation
	Duty
My strategies	*My strategies*
Listen with empathy	Judge, analyse and diagnose
Connect with my feelings and needs	Blame and criticise
Connect with the feelings and needs of others	Make demands and use rewards and punishment
Make do-able requests	Advise, lecture, scold and argue

A real dialogue

'So the thing about anger, right,' said Eric, jabbing his finger at me across the table, 'is that people just don't understand, they don't seem to get that they've overstepped the mark. So they need to know, don't they? They need to be told. It's obvious, innit? Otherwise how are they going to know they've got it wrong?'

His eyes are bulging now, cheeks reddening as his voice takes on a quavering tone. In fact, if I imagine myself taking a few paces back, it seems as if his whole upper body is quavering too.

'Are you feeling angry right now?' I asked.

'What?' he said as if I had stuck a pin in his hand. 'What d'you mean?'

'I mean, are you feeling angry now as you are explaining to me what the point of getting angry is for you?'

'I dunno.' The quavering and reddening lessens as that great double act, reflection and awareness, work their magic.

His face softens and his hard, jabbing pistol-finger lowers towards the table. 'Yes,' he says with surprise in his voice. 'Blimey, I am. What's going on?'

What exactly was going on? There he was, talking to a person who had nothing to do with what happened. How was he able to reproduce his thoughts, feelings and some of his behaviour, even though we were in a different environment and it was weeks after the actual event that he was in the process of describing?

I don't believe Eric was just describing this event as if he were a reporter. He was reliving it as if it were happening all over again. To use an expression from the language of NLP, he was 'fully associated with' his memory. There was no distance or separation between Eric back then and Eric talking to me. I like to think of it as a dream or a film of his own making, in which he has the starring role!

He was so much 'in it' that it came as a shock when I asked him a question. Not because it was a probing or an awkward one, far from it. It was as if I had walked into his private cinema and stopped the film. I'd effectively woken him from his dream. And, like waking up, it had taken several seconds for him to understand what I had asked. His private cinema needed a bit of time to dissolve and be replaced by our actual surroundings.

I'm using the word 'dream', but for Eric, it was more of a nightmare. He was stuck in an unhelpful habit that had become so automatic that it had become very difficult to realise that it was a habit. I wonder if you can identify with what was happening for him, or know other people in your life who have similar experiences.

Another way to understand what is happening is to imagine a deep furrow being created in a field by a plough, which goes up and down the same furrow, making the rut deeper and deeper. Neurologically speaking, this is not far away from what actually happens in our brains by repetitive thoughts and behaviour.

The limitation here is, as the saying goes: 'A rut is merely a grave with the sides kicked out.' For along with habits that we are unaware of can often go the sense of powerlessness or helplessness that accompanies them. 'This is who I am,' we might say, 'and I can't do anything about it. It's just what I do.'

Now a statement like that requires us to stop for a while and pursue some investigation into two key elements in how we experience ourselves in the world. These two elements are power and responsibility.

The drama triangle

The model below is called 'the drama triangle', and was created by Steven Karpman in 1968. He suggests that many of our daily interactions with other people are like a drama in which we play one of three roles named the rescuer, the victim and the perpetrator.

Karpman's original premise was a development of the transactional analysis (TA) model proposed by Eric Berne in the 1960s (Berne, 1964). Berne suggested that in our daily lives we create and use a script just like an actor in a play or film. One of the most popular scripts, suggested Karpman, fits the dramas that get played out by each of these three roles. The roles are based on:

- our concept or beliefs about who we are
- our perception of the world
- how we relate to the world
- how we perceive the world to relate to us
- our perception about how other people treat us.

Our preferred role and its script are based on what each of us is told from an early age, what we experience and what meaning we make of our experiences.

Gary Craig (see references), founder of the emotional freedom technique (EFT), describes this way of making meaning as reading the 'writing on our walls'. What he means is that we are influenced significantly by those people who we are closest to and exposed to from our earliest days. Furthermore, these thoughts, beliefs and attitudes will lie far below our conscious awareness so we can often be blind to these hidden factors that are driving our actions.

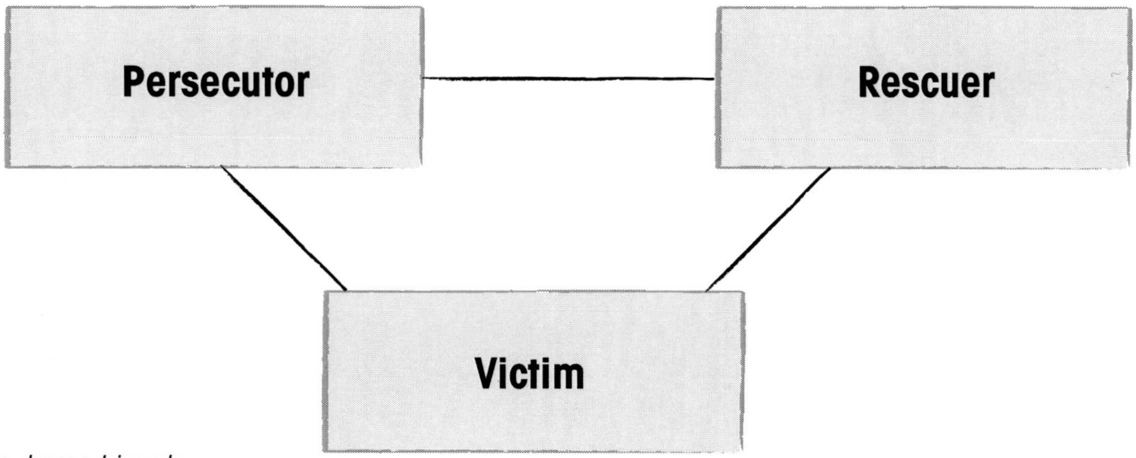

The drama triangle

The roles of the drama triangle

A rescuer is someone who often does not own their own vulnerability and seeks instead to rescue those whom they see as vulnerable.

A rescuer will often do more than their fair share of any work to be done; they may offer help unasked rather than find out whether and how the other person wants to be supported; and what the rescuer agrees to do may not be what they really want to do. This means that the rescuer may then often end up feeling hard done by or resentful, used or unappreciated in some way.

The rescuer does not take personal responsibility, but rather tries to take responsibility for the victim they rescue. The rescuer will frequently end up in the victim position, but may be perceived to be a persecutor by those on the outside looking in.

The underlying attitude of a rescuer can be summed up by such phrases as: 'poor you', 'I'll do it for you', 'you need my help' and 'you can't'.

The actions and attitudes of a rescuer are attempts to fulfil their needs for acceptance, recognition and achievement. These attempts are doomed to fail because they are being done through the lives of other people rather than through the rescuer's own.

A victim is someone who usually feels overwhelmed by their own sense of vulnerability, inadequacy or powerlessness, does not take responsibility for themselves or their own power, and therefore looks for a rescuer to take care of them.

At some point in the drama, the victim may feel let down by their rescuer, or perhaps overwhelmed or even persecuted by them. At this stage the victim will move to the persecutor position, and persecute their rescuer. They may even enlist another rescuer to persecute the previous rescuer. However, the victim will often continue to perceive themselves as the victim.

The underlying attitude of the victim role is best summed up by phrases such as: 'I can't', 'I'll fail', 'I don't know how to' and 'it's my fault'.

The actions and attitudes of a victim are attempts to be cared for and looked after by other people.
The role of persecutor is synonymous with being unaware of one's own power, refusing to own it and therefore discounting it. They will then attempt to use their power over other people in ways that are often destructive.

The underlying attitude of a persecutor can be summed up by phrases such as: 'you have to', 'that's not good enough', 'it's your fault' and 'is that the best you can do?'

The actions and attitudes of a persecutor are attempts to meet their needs for self-worth, personal value and significance. They are unlikely to be successful because they are trying to elevate themselves by putting others down, rather than achieving success in their own right.

So, the drama triangle only works when a person discounts or disowns their personal power. Each of the three roles is actually a different aspect of the victim.

- The rescuer needs to take personal responsibility, connect with their power and acknowledge their vulnerability.
- The victim needs to own their vulnerability, take responsibility and also recognise that they have power and are able to use it appropriately.
- The persecutor needs to own their power, rather than be afraid of it or use it covertly.

What makes the drama triangle so appealing? The clue is in the word 'drama'. What this creates in us is adrenaline, which is an extremely addictive substance. It creates a surge of energy and when it starts to fade, we want to generate more adrenaline to feed our addiction, so increasing our desire for creating drama in our lives. It becomes a vicious circle.

One very effective way to stop the drama and to get out of the triangle is to follow the five-step formula. Once we have developed an awareness of our thoughts, feelings and needs, and can make a request to get those needs met, then the use of roles and scripts, which have been a painful strategy to meet a need, are no longer necessary.

The drama triangle in action

Dad comes home from work to find Mum and son engaged in battle. 'Clean up your room or else,' Mum threatens.

Dad immediately comes to the rescue. 'Mum,' he might say, 'give the boy a break. He's been at school all day.'

Any one of several possibilities might follow.

Perhaps Mum, feeling victimised by Dad, will turn her wrath on him. In that case, Dad is moved from rescuer to victim. They then might do a few quick trips around the triangle with son on the sidelines.

Or maybe son joins Dad in a persecutory 'let's gang up on Mum' approach.

Or then again, maybe son will turn on Dad, rescuing Mum, with: 'Mind your own business, Dad. I don't need your help!'

And so it continues with endless variations, but nonetheless, pinging from corner to corner on the triangle. For many individuals, couples and families, it's the only way they know to interact because we've all been surrounded by this all of our lives.

I'm reminded of an episode of *The Simpsons* where the family agree to attend a family therapy session. Each of them has a box with a button on the top. Each of the boxes is wired to each other and to each member of the family. The idea is that it will help create empathy between them as they realise that a barbed comment, a blaming statement, a label or an insult causes as much pain as an electric shock. What in fact happens is that they realise that they can cause pain by the statement and the electric shock, so create double the pain for each other!

So a technique on its own without a mindset and attitude shift might only make the warring more skilful.

The good news

- Behaviour is learned.
- Expressing anger in certain ways has been learned.
- Because anger expressed in certain learned ways is proving unhelpful to ourselves and to others, those ways can be identified and new, more helpful ways of expressing anger can be learned.

So, let's now find out about other ways you can use to transform your anger non-violently.

Transforming your anger with NLP and EFT

2

Neuro-linguistic programming (NLP)

You may already be familiar with the body of knowledge called neuro-linguistic programming (NLP). By way of a recap, or if it isn't something you know about, I will explain some of the key elements and then describe how I have found it to be a helpful and non-violent way of transforming anger.

NLP began life as a way to meet a need of its co-creators, John Grinder, a mathematician, and Richard Bandler, a linguist. They wanted to satisfy their curiosity. 'How come,' they wondered, 'some healers are really good at what they do?' And when they asked this question to experts in their field – family therapist Virginia Satir and hypnotherapist Milton Erickson – neither of them could answer, other than the vaguest of: 'Well, we just do what we do, ask a few questions that seem right to ask and make a few comments that seem right to make at the time.'

These answers, as you can imagine, did little to meet Grinder and Bandler's need for accurate answers that might help to satisfy their curiosity or help others to learn from these experts.

So they set about sitting in on sessions that these therapists were running to take apart what they were doing and how they were doing it. What they found led to the creation of this body of knowledge called NLP. This seems to be a remarkably robust description and explanation about how we all make sense of the world around us, the meaning we make of the things that happen to us and the way that we communicate both with ourselves internally and with others.

In a nutshell, we humans receive information from the outside world and make sense of this information internally. This is the 'neuro' part of the title.

Essentially, what they realised is that each one of us makes a mental map of reality and then gives information back out to others using that map. In order to 'navigate' our way in life, we need not only our individual 'maps', but also a 'compass' to guide us. The 'linguistic' part of NLP enables us to recognise what our 'map' and 'compass' are.

The actual words that we use, if we listen to them carefully, will indicate which of our five senses we are using to process information, make sense of this information and communicate our experience to others. We will typically have one main sense that we prefer to use, one main 'map' and one preferred 'compass heading'.

For example, if you hear yourself using an expression like 'Do you see what I'm saying?', this suggests that you favour expressing yourself through your sense of sight.

Saying 'What does that sound like?' suggests that you prefer your auditory sense, and 'What's the impact on you of what I'm saying?' is likely to mean that the kinaesthetic (feelings) sense is the one you prefer.

What Grinder and Bandler also realised is that, just like the healers they studied, most people had no conscious awareness of any of this, and, when questioned, were oblivious to what was happening.

So if I refocus your attention on transforming your anger for a moment, the big connection here for me is this:

A problem can be created if you have no idea how you are making sense of the world around you or the things that are happening to you. This can very easily lead you to believe that: 'I just do what I do because that's what I've always done, and surely everybody else thinks, feels, believes and does the same kind of thing too.'

Do you see how this can create problems for us, especially when other people don't do what we ask or expect them to do? These other people may be family members, friends, work colleagues, children, fellow drivers on the road, fellow commuters on the journey to work, people we have voted for or those we have put our trust in to oversee and protect our health or wealth.

Very often, very quickly and very surprisingly, you invite the 'should gang' to visit, especially when you don't even realise you've invited them! They just seem to show up! Our habits are very powerful things. So once you start to realise that there are as many different ways of making sense of the world as there are people in it, you can choose whether this is a real nuisance or a wonderful opportunity.

The nuisance comes as a result of thinking: 'How am I going to work all of this out?'

The wonderful opportunity comes from thinking: 'Wow! Once I find out a bit more about how I'm making sense of my life and what happens to me, it will help me to find out more about how others make sense of their lives and what happens to them'.

'And then, this means that I can communicate more harmoniously with myself and with others than I ever have been able to do before.'

'So, the number of times I'm likely to experience anger at myself (because I'm not accepting what's going on in me, which creates internal conflict) or because I'm angry at another person (because I cannot make a productive or positive connection with them) is highly likely to diminish.'

Whichever thinking you choose, the thing that will empower you is remembering that you have a choice. And this awareness is another great way to get – or stay – out of the drama triangle.

So how do we get to find out about how we make sense of the world around us? I like what author Robert A. Johnson's analyst said when Johnson asked how to find out about psychology: 'Read Greek mythology, read Jung and watch. Watching is best' (Johnson, 2008, p3).

I'd add that it's important not only to watch, but also to listen. By listening to the words that people use (the linguistic part of NLP) you gain a huge amount of information.

For example, if I'm in conversation with a person, every now and again, to check that I'm being understood, I may ask, 'Do you see what I mean?'

And by using this phrase, as opposed to other ones I could have used, for example, 'Do you get what I'm saying?' or 'How's this sounding?', I'm revealing in a very concrete way, by my choice of verb, which of my five senses I prefer to use when I'm talking.

Why not check your own preferences?

If you use a visual or seeing mode, do you 'keep an eye on things', 'see the way ahead clearly', 'look after yourself' and 'take a long-term view of things'?

If the auditory or hearing channel is more for you, then do you 'tune into new ideas', 'maintain harmonious relationships', 'sound people out' and 'keep one ear to the ground'?

Or if the kinaesthetic or feelings channel is more your preference, then do you 'get to grips with new trends', 'keep balance in your life', 'get a feel for things' and 'hold on tight to reality'?

More unusually (statistically speaking), if the olfactory or scent channel is more for you, then you may 'pick up the scent of a scandal', 'turn your nose up at things' and 'smell a rat'.

And lastly, if the taste or gustatory channel calls to you, do you like to 'keep things sweet', 'avoid souring relationships' and 'have exquisite taste in things'?

Now this may be interesting in its own right, but when I have found it to be most valuable is when I'm in dialogue with others.

Why? Because it's in this meeting place between us that communication can become easy and flowing, or awkward and sticky.

Imagine a situation where two people are having a conversation. They could be members of a family or team members in a place of work. Perhaps the conversation goes a little like this:

A: 'Look, I've shown you how to do it countless times and you still don't see what I'm showing you.'
B: 'Well it's a pretty tough thing to grasp when you're throwing all these points at me.'

Do you get what makes this a sticky kind of conversation?

From the example above, person A expresses themselves using some key words that show they prefer the visual channel, whereas for person B the preference is for the kinaesthetic channel. If these two people do not develop an awareness of their preferences, they are likely to have continuing difficulty in communicating.

Imagine how easy it would be for either or both to receive a rapid visit from the 'should gang'. This visit could make itself known by thoughts to describe the other person, such as 'stupid', 'thick', 'slow' or 'inconsiderate'. These are labels that describe how a person *is* rather than what they are doing or saying, and will inevitably lead to an increase in friction between these people, even if the labels are not spoken out loud.

This in turn stimulates our other frequent visitors, 'the three thoughts that fuel anger'. Remember those:

1 how right or clever I am.
2 how wrong or stupid you are.
3 as soon as you agree with me, then everything will be fine.

So, once again, where the 'should gang' can visit rapidly and silently, they can lead us to form swift and flimsily formed opinions and judgements of others and ourselves. These opinions and judgements will reveal themselves as words of accusations and blame, either silently to ourselves or out loud to, or about, others.

This is the flip side of non-violence. In fact, it is the very essence of violence, long before it manifests in any kind of actions that we might typically describe as violent. To spot it requires a change of habit for, as Einstein said, 'You cannot solve a problem with the same kind of thinking that created it.' Or, as the saying goes, 'If you are a worm living in horseradish, all the world is horseradish!'
So if we stay put with what we have always done, we will indeed get what we have always got. However, I am thankful that I have a choice. And so do you.

This is not the wasp sting. If you remember, there is a gap between the stimulus for your anger (what happens outside you), and the cause of it (an 'inside job', based on what you are telling yourself). And that gap is called choice and is what gives you power in the situation.

So the choice is a simple one. You can continue to do what you have been led to do and respond habitually in a way that's likely to provoke the traditional type of anger making, or you can seek to transform the anger non-violently.

As you will realise by now, one of the best ways I have found to do this is to translate the violence of my judgemental, opinionated mind into the thoughts, feelings and unmet needs that are actually at the heart and core of my being, using the five-step formula.

However, using NLP can also help. Going back to the example of the conversation between person A and person B, what non-violent suggestion can be made here to help these two people, who, I believe, long for the kind of easy, respectful communication that we all do?

How about this:

Translation from person B to person A: 'No matter how much A tries to explain this to you, B, she realises that it's hard for you to grasp it.'

Translation from person A to person B: 'B really wants to see eye to eye with you, A, but he needs more time to take in one picture at a time before you show him the next one.'

Or we could choose to use an altogether different, more neutral-channel such as the auditory one: 'So you both want to get through to each other and be heard, but there is still a lot of static on the line that is making it difficult for you to hear each other and sing from the same song sheet.'

Or if they are both aware of their preferred mode of expressing themselves, they could work on it together and end up with a similar outcome. For example, they might arrive at this sort of sentence: 'So we both want to get through to each other and be heard, but there is still a lot of static on the line that is making it difficult for us to hear each other and sing from the same song sheet, yes?'

Of course, this is just a small example of one aspect of this large body of knowledge, so if your appetite has been whetted by any of the above, see how many references on the internet you can grab hold of. There are bound to be some that will be to your taste, and I am sure you will enjoy the sweet smell of the success that comes with more harmonious, flowing conversations. (Did you notice what I just did? I tried to get at least one reference to each sense written here. How did I do? How many did you spot?)

Emotional freedom technique (EFT)

Both NVC and NLP pay attention to the impact our language has on our behaviour and I'd agree that this is a very important aspect of being human. There is another aspect that is equally important, but more difficult to grasp, because it's not so obvious. In fact, it's invisible to the naked eye. I'm referring to the flow of energy that circulates through channels in the body known as meridians. These were first described in the Chinese culture many thousands of years ago. It was known that if the flow of energy along these meridians became blocked or impeded, then illness was a likely consequence. The ancient practice of acupuncture grew out of this understanding. It works by using very thin needles inserted at particular points on the meridians in order to restore our body's natural flow of energy.

What has any of this to do with anger? In the 1990s, Gary Craig developed a method to alleviate physical, mental and emotional problems for people in a rapid, long-lasting and non-violent way. This method is called emotional freedom technique (EFT). It works by identifying an emotional, mental or physical problem, and then tapping firmly on the ends of the major energy meridians.
The science behind this is simple. When we experience a shock or trauma in our lives, it creates a disturbance in our body's energy system. This disturbance shows up as an unhelpful emotion, unwanted behaviour or a painful physical condition.

If you have ever seen a light bulb flickering as a result of a faulty connection, then this is similar to what our bodies experience as a result of such a disturbance. Tapping firmly on a small number of acupressure points allows for the smooth and easy flow of energy to once again circulate around the body. As a result, the unhelpful emotion or painful condition becomes a thing of the past.

Using EFT

The basic premise

All negative emotions are caused by a disruption in the body's energy system.

Before tapping

Using a scale of 0–10, assess the intensity of the feeling associated with the problem.

The set-up phrase

Repeat an affirmation three times while tapping lightly with your index and middle fingers on the 'karate chop' point, which is found on the side of the hand that you would use if you were intending to break a piece of wood in a karate demonstration.

The affirmation goes as follows: 'Even though I have this "x", I deeply and completely accept myself.' For 'x', insert your problem, such as 'headache', 'fear of heights', 'craving for a cigarette' or 'anger at my dad'.
Here are some points worth bearing in mind about using the affirmation.

- It doesn't matter whether you believe the affirmation or not: you just need to say it.
- It works best when you say it with emphasis and conviction, but it works anyway.
- It works best if you say it out loud, but if you are in a situation where that is difficult, saying it under your breath or in your mind does not stop it working.

Tapping the points

Now comes the sequence of tapping on the end of each major energy meridian. It's best to use the index and middle fingers to do the tapping as this covers a wider area than just using one. Tap on these points about seven times while repeating part of the set-up phrase such as 'this headache', 'this anger'.
The points are:

- eyebrow (the end closest to your nose)
- side of the eye (on the bone, not your temple)
- under the eye (in the middle and on the bone)
- under the nose (in the middle between the base of your nose and your top lip)
- above the chin (in the middle between your bottom lip and your chin)
- collar bone (just at the start of your collar bone by the breastbone)
- under the armpit (for females where the bra strap goes and for males in line with your nipple).

After tapping

- Reassess the intensity of your feelings on the 0–10 scale.
- If another round of tapping is required, it's only necessary to tap the points and use the reminder phrase rather than use the set-up phrase again. This time, however, use the phrase 'remaining anger' as you tap.
- Repeat until there is no intensity left. The aim is always to get to a zero.

You can find specific exercises related to transforming your anger with EFT in the Resources section of this book.

Transforming your anger with difficult people

3

Here's a question for you: What's the number one rule for dealing with difficult people? Here's my answer: Don't take it personally!

Why not? Well, it's highly likely that the person who is really making life difficult for you is making life difficult for others too. Would you be willing to step into their shoes for a minute? (How about 30 seconds?)

Can you at all accept that this person, who you will have labelled as an 'x' (you fill in the missing word), is behaving in a way that is inwardly focused, that they are not thinking about you at all or, if they are, it's in relation to achieving their goals? How honest do you want to be right now? Well, I'm saying sorry in advance, but if you don't like this next suggestion, pretend you never read it, OK?

Most people don't think about you. Most people don't care about you.

Let me say that again with a stronger emphasis. Most people on the planet do not care about you. Is this painful to hear? Are you feeling hurt?

You may not agree with the statement, and that's OK. I want it to be different, hence one of my reasons for writing this book, but that's what I believe to be true. Could you perceive difficult people as being an accurate representation of this? The beautiful thing about it is that they behave completely predictably. The trick, the challenge and the skill is to stay free of the strong emotions that can run in an encounter with such a person, and be able to describe what they are focused on. Believe me, they will have a focus!

It may be that attention to detail is their focus (you may label it 'pedantry', 'nit-picking', 'anoraky', and other even less charitable phrases), or they may be very abrupt, looking frequently at their watches or the clock on the wall when they are with you, or perhaps they talk about themselves incessantly, bringing all conversations back to themselves.

Do any of these behaviours seem familiar?

So what to do?

How about: 'Don't argue with reality!'

Meet them in their world. Provide the detail seeker with details. Come straight to the point with the person who is very conscious of using time efficiently.

And what about the person who uses themselves as a constant reference point for all discussions? Acknowledge their achievements!

Notice if, underneath any labels you have given them, you feel a certain exasperation or frustration. Could it be that driving those feelings is a desire for them to be different? And might that be because you have a longing for a certain kind of connection with them that is absent?

I have found it really important to be clear about the outcome I want, and see the above strategies as entry points to conversations that aim to get everyone's needs met. Aiming for a 'win–win' outcome leads to constructive communication. This is not to say that there will be no friction or heat between you and another, but the ultimate aim is to achieve a mutually satisfying outcome.

Aiming to get your own way irrespective of others is highly likely to lead to raised voices, temperature and blood pressure. This, in turn, is highly likely to lead to large helpings of anger, unproductive conflict, simmering resentment leading to revenge, or resignation with an unhealthy side dish full of sighs and eyes rolling to the ceiling.

So, for me, accepting that I am selfish and motivated by self-interest is a tremendous relief. No more pretence or striving to be liked by anyone other than the face that looks back at me from the mirror. Phew, blessed relief indeed.

So what does that mean? That I am the only person that I care about? That nobody cares about anyone else?

Perhaps.

Are we all just going to be cold-blooded and ruthless in our approach to people and situations? And if so, what is the effect on you of that thought? What sort of world does that conjure up? A world that is cold and uncaring?

Or could it be a world where each of us takes increasing responsibility for our own happiness and well-being?

With that comes the freedom that allows you to care out of real care and real love rather than what I term the 'false love' of duty and obligation or because my 'writing on the wall' (see Chapter 4) says that 'I have to be nice, polite, good, thoughtful and considerate of others, because if I don't, no one will like me and I'll be lonely and miserable. Or I will be known as a bad person and suffer the pain of shame, perhaps believing that there is something wrong with me.'

Did you spot the last bit of that sentence?

If that is your motivation for your words and actions, can you honestly say that you were thinking about the other person or, ultimately, weren't you more interested in the effect and consequence for yourself? And how does that make you different from that person you were judging? You remember that person, don't you; the one that drives you to distraction?

Roy Lilley (2002, p16) lists 15 core beliefs that encourage us to get drawn into conflict in angry ways. Notice how many of them have us 'argue with reality'.

Here are just a few for starters – you can read them all in his book and work out which ones are your favourites.

- I must be loved and accepted by everyone.
- I must be perfect in all I do.
- All the people I live and work with must be perfect in all I do.
- I have little power or control over what happens to me.
- People, including me, do not change.
- Disagreements and conflict should be avoided at all costs.
- Some people are always good, some always bad – I need to be good.
- People are fragile and need to be protected, especially from what I really think.
- I should not have problems, or if I do, it proves I'm incompetent.

Phew! I don't know about you, but I feel battered and exhausted just reading these, let alone trying to live them. Notice how many of them have been written by the 'should gang'.

I've found it really helpful and important to work out which beliefs I hold. This has given me the chance to approach a person who I label as 'difficult' in a way that's highly likely to lead to a 'win–win' outcome with little or no anger.

Much of that is because I've embraced and put into practice two key realisations.

Realisation One

First, it's to accept that I have a sphere of concern and a sphere of influence – and that they are different. As you can see from the graphic below, one is much larger than the other.

So I may have concerns about world poverty, global warming, the global economy, and so forth. But what can I actually do about any of it?

If I focus only on my concerns, I could feel overwhelmed by the immensity of it all, and feel helpless and despondent about my powerlessness. Alternatively, I can focus on what I can do – my sphere of influence – and by so doing, develop a sense of achievement and take comfort from what I am able to do, rather than focus on what I am failing to do.

And if the 'law of attraction' holds any attraction for you, then you will know that what you pay attention to increases.

In my experience, paying excess attention to my sphere of concern creates stress, unhappiness and dissatisfaction, whereas paying attention to my sphere of influence, what I can actually do on a day-to-day basis, gives me a sense of purpose and personal empowerment.

I know which I prefer to experience. How about you?

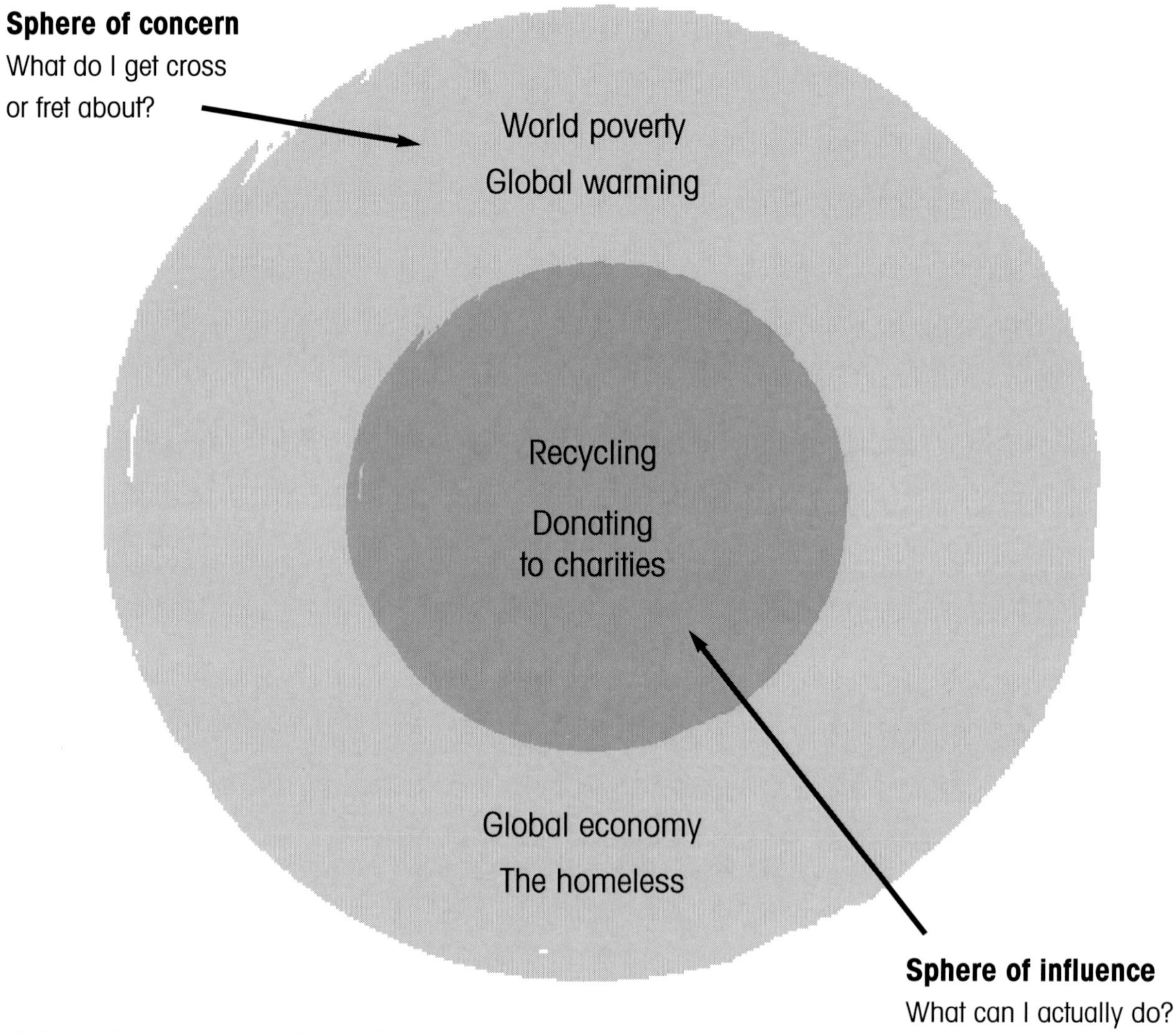

Sphere of concern and sphere of influence

Realisation Two

This realisation has made a great difference to how angry I get with people and situations. It comes from this seemingly simple yet profound statement: 'Accept the reality of what you are experiencing.'

In other words, if someone behaves in a way you don't like, notice if you start a war inside you because the 'should gang' have arrived and you are telling yourself: 'They shouldn't be treating me like this.' The reality is that they are treating you like this! Accept the reality of this!

'Hang on!' you might be thinking. 'Isn't this a recipe for being a doormat? For being treated in ways I'm really not going to enjoy?'
My answer is: 'No.'

For as soon as the war stops in you, your blood pressure remains steady, you feel a sense of equilibrium so that you are on an even keel, and you're not thrown upside down and inside out internally. Then – guess what?

You are no longer responding in the way you used to.

And now you can use the five-step formula:

Step 1: What's happening?

Step 2: Notice whether any of your thoughts have been sent to you from the 'should gang'? If so, then my advice is to translate them into feelings and needs before you say a word out loud.

Step 3: Say what you are feeling.

Step 4: Say what you are needing.

Step 5: State a do-able request aimed at getting your needs met.

And double guess what? It's highly likely that the person or the situation will begin to transform before your very eyes.

Or you may want to use steps 3, 4 and 5 as questions to the other person, as in this example:
'Are you feeling "x" because you need "y"? And what would you like now in order to meet that need?'

Why not try it?

My advice, based on my own experience, is to try it on a person or situation that has just a bit of a challenge for you, rather than go for that which is most difficult.

Now it's back to one of the central points of this book, namely that anger is an 'inside job', and related entirely to your perception of events, the meaning you make of those events and what you do as a result of that meaning.

So it may not be that the people or situations are any less bothersome, but that the meaning you make of them is different. And you may not feel angry any more, but you may be feeling something else.

If you want a more direct alternative or even an antidote to the list of unhelpful beliefs above, read the following list and notice whether you feel any different at the end compared with how you felt after the list of beliefs.

Ten commandments for reducing stress

1 Thou shalt not be perfect, or even try to be.
2 Thou shalt not try to be all things to all people.
3 Thou shalt leave things undone that ought to be done.
4 Thou shalt not spread thyself too thinly.
5 Thou shalt learn to say 'no'.
6 Thou shalt schedule time for thyself, and for thy supportive network.
7 Thou shalt switch off and do nothing regularly.
8 Thou shalt be boring, untidy, inelegant and unattractive at times.
9 Thou shalt not even feel guilty.
10 Thou shalt not be thine own worst enemy, but be thy best friend.

Do you feel any different?

I found this piece a long time ago. I can't remember where I got it, so apologies and thanks to you if you're the author. I keep it secured by magnets to my fridge door. I look at it every now and then. It helps.

A bigger picture of anger

I have included an idea from Michael Meade (1993), who puts forward a perspective on the place and role of anger. This speaks well to me. I wonder how it resonates with you? I'll represent it graphically and then explain my understanding of what he suggests.

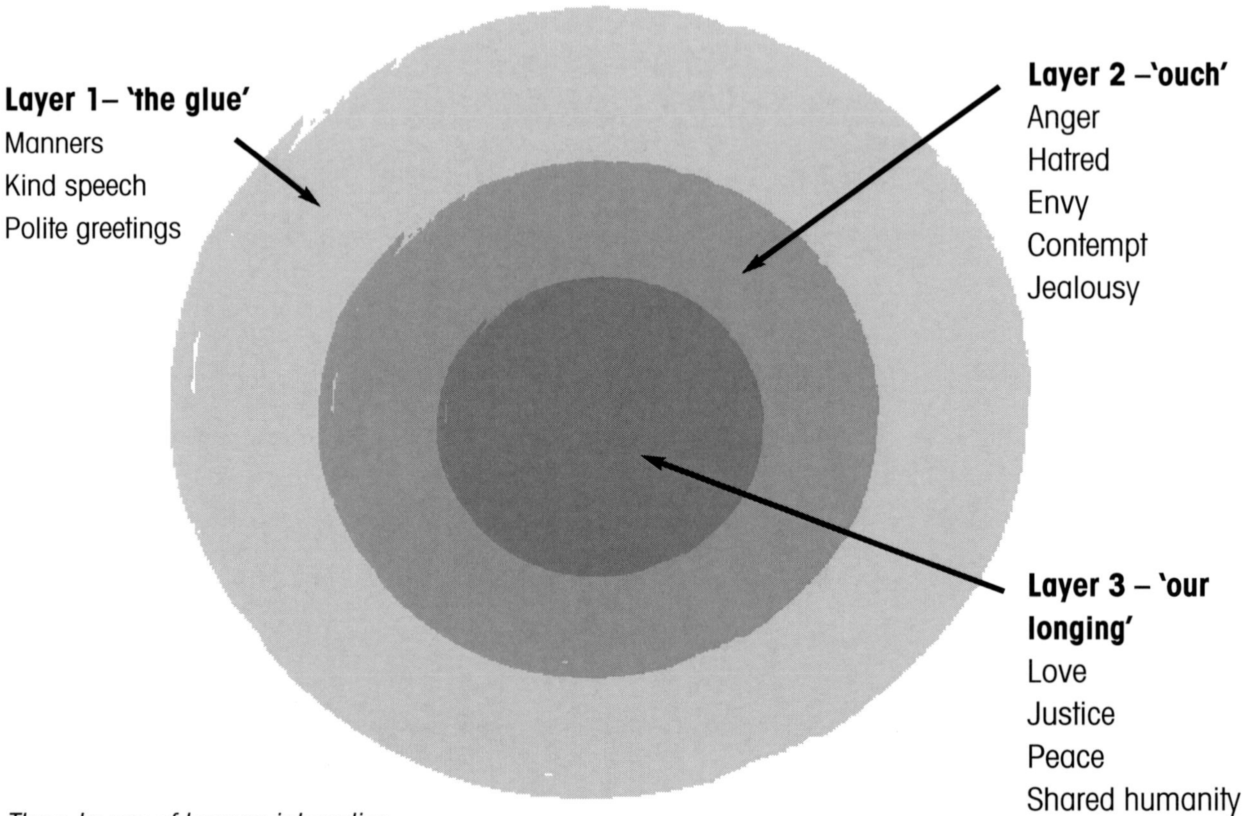

Three layers of human interaction

So the first layer represents that place where we meet others in a day-to-day social environment and what we say makes 'life in passing' possible. For example, the expression 'How are you?' is a way that many English speaking people in the so-called developed world understand is like a secret, coded message. The reply is, of course, 'Fine', 'Not bad', 'OK' or some such phrase. This confirms that you are members of the same 'club' and you both know the passwords!

Imagine if you started to tell the person who had asked 'How are you?' the truth! 'Well, to be honest, I'm really not very happy right now. You see, I haven't made love with my …'

Do you imagine that the person who asked you is still there at the water cooler or the coffee machine? Even if their body is there, they will have left the building at an early point in your reply! So the 'code' and the 'club membership' are about being in agreement with each other about what the rules are. And agreeing the rules creates a certain type of order, which creates a type of safety and predictability rather than uncertainty about how to behave.

If you were to visit an African country, the greeting you received might be very different, and I don't mean just the language. You might hear 'Tell me your story', which is a genuine way of connecting with you, a genuine desire to know what is happening for you in your life.

A wider point here relates to concepts of time. It may well be that one of the rules that you live by is this: there are only 24 hours in a day and you have a number of tasks to do in that time, some of which you get paid to do. If you don't get those tasks done, you will feel anxious or irritated. So if someone asks you how you are and you begin to tell them, you start to feel anxious about spending time talking rather than 'getting on'. Whereas, for a person living in a village with no clock, there are still things to be done, and it is these very events that shape how time is measured and spent. So you may need to sweep, to clean, to hunt, to cook and to sit and converse, none of which you get paid to do, but those are the rules that you are living by, and sitting and conversing is a vital part of community building. And building community is a vital part of your life, so it makes absolute sense to devote time on a daily basis to sharing how you and others are.

Let's return to the three layers.

The first layer is vital for social survival, to enable us to function confidently and consistently. However, if we spend too much time here, a menacing shadow begins to grow in the second layer. More of this shortly.

The third layer is the province of deep unity with all things and with the great themes and images of life. Without some experience of this layer, we die. Societies, alliances, relationships and individual souls must occasionally fall into these pools of unity or else they dry out or blow up.

When we 'fall in love', it's the ground of the third layer we fall on. In this place, 'all you need is love' and 'love is all there is'. Finally, 'justice is served' and the wrongs are righted. And for a moment, 'all is right with the world'.

This layer is where the images of god exist, where prayers are answered, where healing mends the wounds of life, where peace becomes real and contagious.

'Visualise world peace' is a third-layer bumper sticker, as are 'Jesus loves you' and 'This car stops for ducks'.

We all want to be in the warmth and peace of the third layer. All utopias reside here. We mount great efforts to get there through meditation and prayer, through great social movements and through working at our relationships.

We can sit there rent-free and see how it was all worth it. In the clear skies and fresh air of the third layer we can truly forgive the insults, punishments and injustices heaped on us. Here at the depths, a rare stream of humour cleanses the old wounds and makes our eyes bright for life.

Here's the bad news: The third layer is constantly moving in location. It's not to be found today where it was found yesterday. We can go through the motions, exactly repeating everything that previously got us to that state of peace, love and bliss, and this time – we get nowhere. The third layer is mysterious and unpredictable and leaves no forwarding address.

This is different from the first layer, which is always in the same place – it is certain and predictable, albeit superficial.

The second layer

Can you read the signs written here? 'Beware of the dog'; 'Get a life'; 'S*** happens'.

The second layer says, 'I can't take it any more, I won't stand for it, I've had enough.'

The second layer sends postcards from hell and greetings from the underworld. 'How about a nice, special delivery order of rage pie, a fillet of hatred, a salad of jealousy and a plate of envy and wrath?'

It is a stove that seethes with an adverse, acidic, acrid and angry stew. This is a stew that bubbles with feelings, emotions and attitudes we'd rather not have, wouldn't choose and shouldn't express. Under the surface can be minor tremors that rattle a few dishes and then subside; or there can be the equivalent of earthquakes that shatter, rend and collapse whatever has been built up above.

The population of the second layer includes a high percentage of giants, hags, trolls, boxers, bears, street criminals, cops, vultures, gargoyles, streetwalkers and outraged motorists. The pavements in this area are cracked, the stores are closed, the lights don't work and there is no one who will listen to you. Cultures that try to shut out this second layer, whether in a family, school, workplace or neighbourhood, wind up with overcrowded prisons, high crime rates, huge black markets and, finally, riots on the streets.

Enough bad news? Sorry, not quite finished yet.

The only way out of the first layer, the only way to break the spell of niceness, is to enter the turmoil of the second layer and spend some time there. Furthermore, the only way to find the next location of the third layer is by traversing the battle-scarred, dog-infested terrain of the second layer.

Or, as poets William Blake and Emily Dickinson would have it:

> I was angry with my friend:
> I told my wrath, my wrath did end.
> I was angry with my foe:
> I told it not, my wrath did grow.
> (William Blake, 'A poison tree')
>
> Anger as soon as fed is dead;
> 'Tis starving makes it fat.
> (Emily Dickinson, 'Mine enemy is growing old')

Quoted in Bly *et al*, 1993, pp302 and 304)

So, if you are willing to accept that the only way to reach the third layer, the one that we all long for, is through the 'dog-infested' terrain of the second layer, then don't be surprised if people who you find difficult pop Into your life. Could it be that they are offering you a chance to navigate your way from the first to the third layer? And when you make such a journey, doesn't it make even more sense to carry the best kind of equipment?

I am sure it will come as no surprise to learn that my recommendation to you is to ensure that your non-violent equipment is with you at all times!

Transforming your anger in the family

4

I think that it is really important that we as parents demonstrate not only love and 'common sense' but also skill.

There is no doubt in my mind that parenting of and caring for youngsters is one of the hardest, if not the hardest, job there is.

And, in my opinion, there's no earthly reason why anybody would be any good at it, for what have most of us based our own parenting style and actions on? Typically, we will be either copying or rebelling against how we ourselves were parented. And while I mean no disrespect to my mum and dad, their parenting left quite a lot to be desired.

I'd like to think that I did a better job (but you'd have to ask Jack, Ross and Louie about that), and while that may have been generally true, that dent in the plasterboard wall on the landing caused by my 'fist of anger' with Ross told me that I still had a bit to learn!

What I have learned since then is what I'd like to share with you.

I believe that what I have learned will make me a better grandparent than I was a parent (but you'll have to ask Harley and my other, as yet unborn, grandchildren about that). And I'm expecting that what I have learned will help my sons to be better fathers than I was, and so on into the future.

So what is it that I have learned?

Well, thanks to the work of people like Haim Ginott (you will meet him later) and Marshall Rosenberg, I've learned that when we're communicating with youngsters, it's very important to pay attention to what they are thinking, feeling and needing, rather than paying attention only to what they are doing and saying.

This is simple to write and 'know', but not always so easy to do, especially when (1) our longstanding habits of many years, and the habits of all the people around us, reinforce the 'traditional way' of doing things; and (2) youngsters often talk in 'code'.

As a consequence of paying attention to and finding out what they are thinking, feeling and needing, one significant change for me is the amount of time I spend listening as opposed to talking. As a rough guide, I use the Pareto principle, or the so-called '80/20' rule, to help me monitor how much talking and listening I'm doing in a conversation.

The '80/20' rule is the suggestion that 80 per cent of our results come from 20 per cent of our endeavours – so it's really helpful to work out which 20 per cent creates the real results! So, if I want to find out what a youngster is thinking, feeling and needing, I'm seeking to talk for only 20 per cent of the total time of the conversation and listen for 80 per cent. This is actually a principle I hold to about listening to people in general, not just to youngsters.

One of the hardest things I had to grasp, and I would say it's true for the vast majority of adults I teach and coach, is that 'listening is doing'. Let me explain.

I have not yet met a parent who does not want the best for their child, who does not want to feel a sense of pride in who their child is and what their child is doing, both now and when they grow up. Now, there may be parents who don't want these things for their children, but I have not come into contact with them. And I choose to believe that, if they exist, they are very few and far between. And in wanting the best for our children, we perhaps believe that there are certain things that we need to do to help them. Things like offering them advice, suggestions and solutions when they haven't asked for that kind of help. Or that scolding or criticising them will help them to learn from their mistakes or perhaps save them from making mistakes in the first place. Or perhaps we have become tired of fighting and have given in and given up because it's just too darned tough to have another row.

Choices and habits

I'm suggesting that we actually have four choices about how we respond to another person's actions, but the approach described by the word 'Restorative' in the top right box below is the one that asks us to express our thoughts, feelings and needs and to hear those of others.

Discipline Limit – setting Boundaries	High	Authoritarian (To)	Restorative (With)
		Neglectful (Not)	Permissive (For)
	Low		High
		Nurture Care Support	

Our four choices

Let me just check something with you.

What kind of response did you typically receive as a youngster yourself?

I'm willing to wager that it was mostly in one of the three other boxes.

And just how effective was it? How much did it help? How much notice did you take of those suggestions, that advice, that criticism or that lack of interest and attention to you?

Perhaps it worked every time like a lucky charm for you and you are doing exactly the same and it's working brilliantly for you and your children. In which case, great stuff! Keep on doing it!

If, however, you didn't find these responses very helpful, or found them to be no help at all or to even be counterproductive, it may be that you are open now to listening more carefully to the thoughts, feelings and needs of your own children.

By the way, a big clue about how effective you found any of the other responses is to ask yourself about the quality of relationships that you have now with your parents or, if they are no longer alive, what the quality of your relationship with them was like in their final years.

So, when I wanted to communicate with my kids in a more authentic way, another thing that I found helpful was to be able to identify what my typical style around conflict was. It's often when there are disagreements between people in a family, at work, in a social or interest group or in a neighbourhood that anger shows itself.

I use the word 'edge' to describe those places where we rub up against others in a way that causes friction. Such edges can be sharp and cutting if we use them on each other as ways only to get our needs met. But they can also be used as a new way of understanding others and ourselves.

Written below are the names of five types of creature.

As you read them, just notice whether you are drawn towards one more than another.

- Teddy bear (I know it's not strictly a creature, but just humour me)
- Turtle
- Shark
- Owl
- Fox

Remember a time when you got angry with family members or they got angry with you and there was conflict. Perhaps it was about things like bedtime, time to come in, chores around the house, time to get up and time to get to school, college, work, and so on. Just choose a few examples.

High	Shark		Owl
Goals		Fox	
	Turtle		Teddy bear
Low		**Relationships**	High

Which creature are you?

Now look at the graph above. Notice the words by the horizontal and vertical lines: 'High' and 'Low', and 'Goals' and 'Relationships'.

What I'm suggesting is that if we place a high emphasis on achieving our goals with little regard for the consequences to relationships with those close to us (the top left-hand area of the chart), then there is likely to be friction, or an 'edge', especially if another member of the family is choosing to behave in the same way. The things we think, say and do to put us in this place are all behaviours that are described as 'shark' behaviours.

Can you suggest what sort of things are said and done? Can you remember any occasions when 'shark' behaviour was present?

If, however, you 'run for the hills', take cover, wish the anger and conflict weren't happening and generally 'disappear' in some form, then you are behaving in 'turtle style' and would find yourself in the bottom-left hand area of the chart, with low or negligible interest in achieving a personal goal and in protecting or maintaining a relationship. In short, you wish that whatever was happening was not happening!

Again, you may wish to remember or imagine what is said and done, and how exactly, when you or any one you know behaves in this way.

Hands up the teddy bears! How are you behaving here? Keeping the peace at all costs underpins this way of behaving, so 'fixing' things is uppermost in your mind. 'What can I do for you to make the situation better?' will be some of the thinking here. Making suggestions and offering solutions, providing answers, doing things for someone else, such as giving someone a lift, packing their bag, lending them some money. The key things to note here are repetition and resentment.

Are you finding yourself doing and saying the same thing and feeling resentful about it because the other person is leaning on you more and more? Welcome to the land of the teddy bear! It means putting your own ambition, goals, wants and needs to one side for the sake of the other(s), with the mistaken belief that it will benefit the relationship.

But what kind of relationship will this create? And at whose expense?

Were you drawn to the fox? That would put you pretty much in the middle of the chart, meaning that you are aware of your own goals, what you want to achieve, as well as being aware of the importance of those relationships that mean something to you. So you may be using 'trade-offs' as ways to deal with conflict and anger: 'I'll do this for you if you'll do that for me.'

It will be pretty obvious where the owl goes. And what this means is that there will be a strong desire to arrive at a mutually acceptable, 'win–win', outcome, achieved by holding what may seem to be a paradox. How can you hold on to your personal goals and value highly the relationships with others?

Well, it will come as no surprise that to use the five-step formula here will address everybody's needs, remembering that the purpose of dialogue here is to arrive at a win–win outcome. And do you see a connection between the four choices diagram and this one?

Cracking the code

Another added challenge for parents is that children's communications can often be in some form of code that needs cracking. In caring for them, it's helpful if we understand what the code is and, of course, how to crack it.

Our typical responses may be like the conversation that would take place between two creatures who live on different planets. For example, when my son Louie was nine, he would often be reluctant to go along to a basketball club, which we all knew he enjoyed when he got there. The conversation between him and me would typically go something like this:

L: 'I'm not sure if I want to go to basketball.'

P: 'Oh come on, Louie, it'll be fine. You know you'll enjoy it when you get there.'

L: 'Well, I dunno. Maybe I won't go today. I'll go next week.'

P: 'Nah, c'mon. We'll have the same conversation next week. Let's just go. If we don't go soon, we'll be late.' (My tension is starting to show in my tone, which he notices.)

L: 'Well, I dunno, I've got a stomach ache too.'

And so the conversation would go on, sometimes for quite a while. Sometimes, I'd start to feel angry because (as I now realise, using the understanding that NVC has given me), I was telling myself that he would enjoy it when he got there and why did he not understand or remember that from the last time? So my tone of voice would change and become one that Louie recognised as 'that tone', which just made things worse by creating more anxiety and irritation in him, so making him even more reluctant to go. Does any of this sound familiar to you?

Fast-forward to the present day, and although we're both older now, the way I've learned to respond to such a situation now is highly likely to elicit a different response. So a very similar situation occurred recently when, after several years of not playing, Louie wanted to join a men's basketball club.

The conversation had a very similar starting point:

L: 'I'm not sure I want to go to basketball.'
P: 'Go on. Say a bit more.'
L: 'Well, I haven't played for quite a while and I'm not very fit. These guys are playing regularly.'
P: 'So you're feeling a bit nervous? Unsure how you'll measure up to the others?'
L: ' Yeah.' (Pause). 'I mean, I know it'll be OK when I get there.'

Did I tell him that? Or has he worked it out? Well, it's partly because he's older, of course. But the most important thing for me to pay attention to is what I am doing differently. Did you notice how I've learned to become a pretty good codebreaker? And so can you! Just in case it's not obvious, let me spell out what differences I notice.

First, I am willing to listen, rather than countering his concerns with positive statements. I used to believe this was helpful, but now realise that it disconnects me from the person. The listening includes silences when neither of us was saying anything.

Second, while I am listening to the words, I'm remembering that they only make up 7 per cent of any communication.

Yes, really!

The other 93 per cent is made up of just two other elements.

The image I use is of the words being a tiny island that sits in a vast ocean.

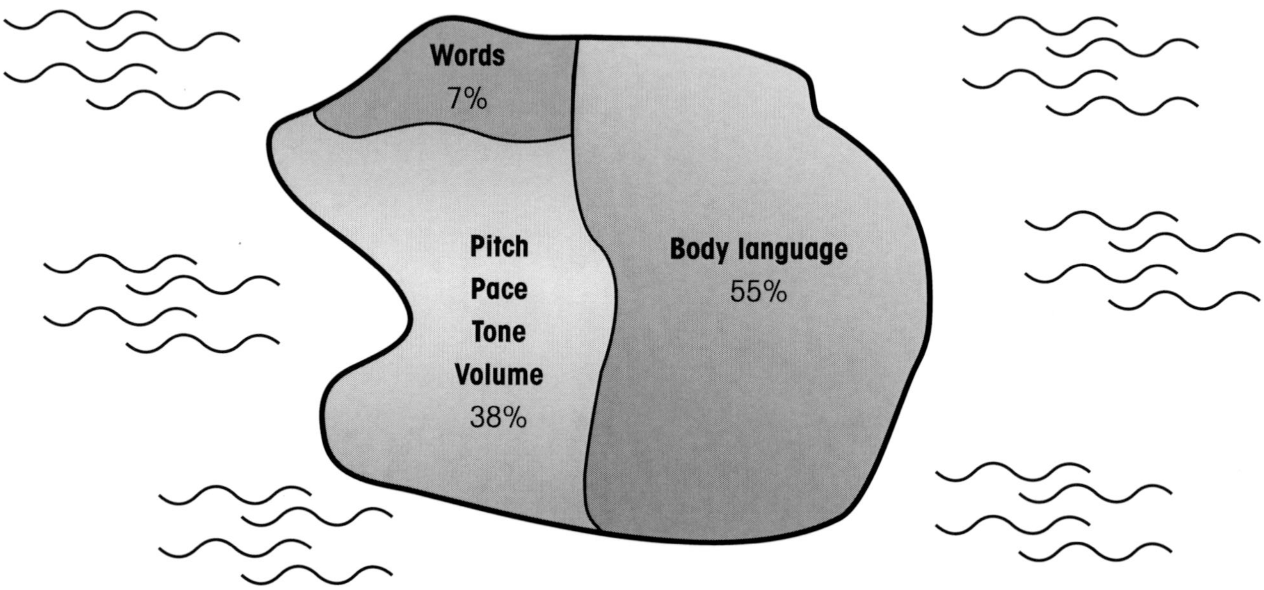

Communication island

Thirty-eight per cent of the total communication is how we're delivering the words: tone of voice, pitch, speed of speech and volume.

Fifty-five per cent is the message that our bodies give: eye contact, how upright we are standing, our sitting posture, our hand gestures, the look on our faces, and so on. And, of course, we are virtually blind to the messages that the 93 per cent are conveying, because we are 'this side of our eyes'! So, returning to my two conversations with Louie, although they started out in virtually identical fashion, my response was simply yet powerfully different, which meant that he worked things out for himself. These are just two examples of thousands of conversations that I, and those I have taught, are using daily in their families and places of work.

In the first example, before I'd learned to 'crack the code', I was coming at things purely from a place of cajoling, persuading and trying to put a 'positive spin' on things, albeit with the best of intentions. If he had not enjoyed basketball, but I thought it would be 'good for him', I would have needed to ask myself the crucial question: 'Whose need is being met by insisting he goes?' So I've embraced the concept and the practice that 'listening is doing', and, further still, by 'cracking the code', I've learned to uncover 'hidden treasure', which lies in the 93 per cent of communication island. So what is this treasure of which I speak? Yes, you've probably guessed that the treasure is our thoughts, feelings and needs. The truth of us.

Our internal world, lying under the ocean's surface.

And what is the best way to access this swirling, magical world where all is murky and unclear? The 'code book' suggests the following steps.

1 Listen to whoever is speaking with an attitude of curiosity and acceptance, even if what's said is normally something you might object to, or have strong personal feelings and beliefs about (this usually takes a bit of practice!).
2 Be patient and let someone's story emerge. Sometimes this may mean saying nothing, just being silent or saying very few words, perhaps 'mmm', 'I see', 'go on', 'say a bit more' and other such phrases.
3 When under water, submarines have found sonar to be helpful. Based on the techniques that certain creatures use, a single sound, a 'ping', is sent out and, if it makes contact with any solid object, the 'ping' sound is returned. This allows the creature to navigate its way in an environment that is murky, unclear or pitch black. Being under the emotional ocean surface can be the same sort of experience. So we can use the same kind of technique by picking up on the last word or two of what someone says, and 'pinging' it back with a lift in the tone of our voice so that it becomes a question. For example, the person I am listening to might say:
   'So I went there on my own …'
   I would pick up on the exact words they had used, then do my best to make sure I made my response a question by saying, 'On your own?'

What are the thoughts and feelings that are emerging by listening to the island and the whole ocean? With Louie, it was clear to me that he was feeling nervous.

Here is a habit that I have got into that I've found really valuable. As soon as I say the words 'I'm feeling', the very next word I use is a word that describes a feeling, such as 'nervous', 'happy' or 'angry'.

Likewise, when anyone says to me 'I was feeling …', I'm listening intently for the next word. Often, because of the way we have been educated, what is said is something like, 'I feel that it's not fair'. When I hear the word 'that', I know I'm hearing an opinion rather than a feeling.

I'll also quite often hear 'I'm feeling like she's always picking on me'. Again, I'm hearing what the person is thinking. My way of responding to this is to ask something like, 'So what's the feeling inside?' or 'And when she's always picking on you, what are you feeling?' And what we are feeling is invariably a clue to the real treasure that sits at the heart of us, just like the 'anger onion' – our needs.

Why do I call these thoughts, feelings and needs 'buried treasure'? Because for me this is where the 'real deal', the real truth of us as people lives.

And most of the time we keep these aspects of us hidden for fear of being hurt again, of repeating past painful experiences. So, not for the first time, our past is indeed 'running our present', and unless we understand this for ourselves, and as parents, unless we can bring this understanding to our encounters with our children, we are unlikely to feel safe enough to talk openly and honestly. This, of course, works both ways.

Here I agree with the words of Karen Casey, when she says: 'Most kids hear what you say, some kids do what you say, but all kids will do what you do'. (Casey, 2006).

I am including a short piece by Haim Ginott to illustrate this point further. Haim Ginott came to this realisation after working as a teacher in Israel, before moving to the USA and becoming one of the foremost family therapists of his era.

Although the piece refers to 'teachers' and 'classroom', for me, it translates just as well if I substitute the word 'parent' and 'home'.

See what you think:

> I've come to the frightening conclusion that I am the decisive element in the classroom. It is my daily mood that makes the weather.
>
> As a teacher, I possess a tremendous power to make a child's life miserable or joyous.
> I can be a tool of torture, or an instrument of inspiration.
> I can humiliate or humour, hurt or heal.
>
> In all situations, it is my response that decides whether a crisis will be escalated or de-escalated, and a child humanised or de-humanised.
> (Ginott, 1975, p13)

In other words, we model behaviours that our children will copy – for good or ill. So I'm not surprised when my sons do and say things that I recognise as direct copies of my words and actions. Have you ever had the experience that when you say something to your child, you hear the voice, tone and intonation of one of your own parents? And you wonder, 'Where did that come from? I swore I'd never say or do that!'

So I realised that to do things differently would require some awareness of what I was doing and saying, whether it was really an authentic statement that I was making or just reading off what Gary Craig, creator of EFT, calls 'the writing on my wall'?

I included a thorough explanation earlier in the book (Chapter 2) of how EFT can help you deal easily, effectively and non-violently with unhelpful anger, and many other obstacles to living non-violently.

I think it's helpful at this stage to explain the meaning of this expression 'writing on the walls' more fully. What Gary Craig suggests is that our internal world is like a room in which we live all of the time. It represents our comfort zone. In this room, writing covers every wall. Some of the writing is big and bold and gets our attention frequently. Other writing is less easy to read, perhaps smaller or fainter, but it's there nevertheless. And It was written there by people such as parents, grandparents, uncles, aunts and teachers, those figures of authority that played an influential role in our lives, especially our early lives. Unless we become aware of what the writing is and how it affects our words and actions, we not only restrict our own freedom of thought, belief, words and actions, but can also provoke a reaction or response from others, especially those closest to us, which can disappoint us, confuse us, take us by surprise, shock or distress us.

For example, if I have writing on my wall (which I now call a belief) which says, 'I have to be on time for meetings and appointments' and that is what got written there by one of my parents, can you imagine the conflict that is waiting for me if my child does not have that same writing on their wall but has different writing?

I can easily make the mistake of using words that the 'should gang' offer to us so freely, telling my child that they are 'lazy', 'disorganised', 'thoughtless', 'inconsiderate', and such like. How much better to use the five-step formula:

- describing the behaviour that I see or hear, as if I were recording it with a camera and microphone
- becoming aware of my thoughts and translating them if necessary, from their judgement into feelings and needs
- expressing my feelings
- expressing my needs
- making a 'do-able' request.

It has been my experience that there will be consequences that nobody is likely to enjoy if I choose the well-grooved path that the 'should gang' offer me.

I'm reminded of what Marshall Rosenberg (Rosenberg, 2000) said about his own children, which brought one of those wry smiles to my lips. You know, when you read or hear something that is funny and awkwardly true at the same time.

He said:

> I'll be forever grateful to my children for educating me about the limitations of the objective of getting other people to do what you want. They taught me that, first of all, I couldn't make them do anything. I couldn't make them put a toy back in the toy box. I couldn't make them make their bed. I couldn't make them eat. Now that was quite a humbling lesson for me as a parent, to learn about my powerlessness, because somewhere I had gotten it into my mind that it was the job of a parent to make a child behave. And here were these young children teaching me this humbling lesson, that I couldn't make them do anything. All I could do is make them wish they had!
>
> And whenever I would be foolish enough to do that, that is to make them wish they had, they taught me a second lesson about parenting and power that has proven very valuable to me over the years. And that lesson was that anytime I would make them wish they had, they would make me wish I hadn't made them wish they had. Violence begets violence.

When I read this first, it got me thinking about what my role was in regard to parenting, and I was very influenced by two other offerings from NVC.

The first spoke directly to me about the purpose of parenting (and teaching). It asks, 'What do we want from our children? Is it obedience, or the development of a will?'

The second offering concerned the use of punishment and rewards in order to get children to do what we want and the honest answers to two questions.

First, what do we want your child to do differently to what they are doing now? Now if we just ask this question, then it is possible to see how punishment (pain), or the threat of it, and rewards (bribes), or the offer of them, might influence a child to do what we want.

But add a vital second question, and the twin strategies of punishment and rewards fail every time. What do you want the child's reasons to be for acting as we would like them to act?

And if I am honest with myself, I realise that the type of relationship I want with my children and what I want for them is hindered rather than helped by the use of punishments and rewards.

I behave more and more like that shark on the diagram if I use punishment and rewards, and there is something about the eyes of a shark I'm not too fond of. Would I want my children seeing that in my eyes every time they look at me?

And if the only alternative was to behave like a teddy bear, and let children do what they wanted, when and where they wanted and however they wanted, well, that would not work for me either.

Fortunately, as you are realising, there are other ways to communicate, which are highly likely to generate a cooperative, collaborative style and a harmonious and fun atmosphere that can be enjoyed by all.

Resources

RESOURCES

Contents

1 How to know what you're feeling

At first glance, this may seem a strange title, but I have lost count of the number of people I encounter who can often struggle to know what they are feeling or what name to give it.

Certainly, the lists of feelings words elsewhere in these resources will help, but what can you do if you haven't the words? How can you truly know what you are feeling?

My answer is invariably the same. And it may seem too simple to believe.

It is this: Ask your body.

Here's a method that works easily and effectively:

1 Close your eyes and start to notice your breathing.
2 Let your breathing get a little slower and deeper.
3 Now let your attention move from the top of your head, slowly scanning down to your neck and shoulders, on down to your chest and upper back, down to your stomach and abdomen.
4 Notice if any of those areas are feeling tight, tense or sore.
5 If you are not sure, just spend a few seconds more scanning again from the top of your head down to your abdomen.
6 Notice three areas in particular:
   - your upper back, neck and shoulders
   - your throat and chest
   - your stomach and abdomen.

Although we have developed language, a much older and reliable way to gauge what we are feeling is held in the body, which belongs to a much older way of working out what we feel. And these three areas of the body typically tell us what we are feeling.

If you notice tension in your upper back, neck or shoulders, the chances are that you are feeling angry.

If you notice tension in your throat or chest, the chances are that you are feeling sadness or longing.

And tension in the third area, your stomach or abdomen, means that you are likely to be feeling scared.

Try it out. It takes very little time. And I have found it to be super-reliable.

And then, of course, you can apply the five-step formula, EFT, NLP or any other non-violent technique that you have learned or know already.

2 List of feelings

The following are words we use when we want to express a combination of emotional states and physical sensations. This list is neither exhaustive nor definitive. Feel free to use the words and add your own.

Feelings when your needs are satisfied

AFFECTIONATE
compassionate
friendly
loving
open-hearted
sympathetic
tender
warm

CONFIDENT
empowered
open
proud
safe
secure

ENGAGED
absorbed
alert
curious
engrossed
enchanted
entranced
fascinated
interested
intrigued
involved
spellbound
stimulated

INSPIRED
amazed
awed
wonder

EXCITED
amazed
animated
ardent
aroused
astonished
dazzled
eager
energetic
enthusiastic
giddy
invigorated
lively
passionate
surprised
vibrant

EXHILARATED
blissful
ecstatic
elated
enthralled
exuberant
radiant
rapturous
thrilled

GRATEFUL
appreciative
moved
thankful
touched

HOPEFUL
expectant
encouraged
optimistic

JOYFUL
amused
delighted
glad
happy
jubilant
pleased
tickled

PEACEFUL
calm
clear-headed
comfortable
centred
content
equanimous
fulfilled
mellow
quiet
relaxed
relieved
satisfied
serene
still
tranquil
trusting

REFRESHED
enlivened
rejuvenated
renewed
rested
restored
revived

Feelings when your needs are not satisfied

AFRAID
apprehensive
dread
foreboding
frightened
mistrustful
panicked
petrified
scared
suspicious
terrified
wary
worried

ANGRY
enraged
furious
incensed
indignant
irate
livid
outraged
resentful

ANNOYED
aggravated
disgruntled
dismayed
displeased
exasperated
frustrated
impatient
irked
irritated

AVERSION
animosity
appalled
contempt
disgusted
dislike
hate
horrified
hostile
repulsed

CONFUSED
ambivalent
baffled
bewildered
dazed
hesitant
lost
mystified
perplexed
puzzled
torn

DISCONNECTED
alienated
aloof
apathetic
bored
cold
detached
distant
distracted
indifferent
numb
removed
uninterested
withdrawn

DISQUIET
agitated
alarmed
disconcerted
disturbed
perturbed
rattled
restless
shocked
startled
surprised
troubled
turbulent
turmoil
uncomfortable
uneasy
unnerved
unsettled
upset

EMBARRASSED
ashamed
chagrined
flustered
guilty
mortified
self-conscious

FATIGUE
beat
burnt out
depleted
exhausted
lethargic
listless
sleepy
tired
weary
worn out

PAIN
agony
anguished
bereaved
devastated
grief
heartbroken
hurt
lonely
miserable
regretful
remorseful

SAD
dejected
depressed
despair
despondent
disappointed
discouraged
disheartened
forlorn
gloomy
hopeless
melancholy
unhappy
wretched

TENSE
anxious
distraught
distressed
edgy
fidgety
frazzled
irritable
nervous
overwhelmed
restless

VULNERABLE
fragile
guarded
helpless
insecure
reserved
sensitive
shaky

YEARNING
envious
jealous
longing
nostalgic
pining
wistful

Source: Center for Non-violent Communication (2005a).

3 List of needs

As with the feelings list, use this list when finding out what your needs are in any given situation and when using the five-step formula. Do add others that are important to you and are not there.

Autonomy	Celebration	Integrity	Creativity	Acceptance
Community	Contribution	Honesty	Love	Meaning
Respect	Safety	Support	Trust	Play
Beauty	Harmony	Order	Peace	

Source: Center for Non-violent Communication (2005b).

4 The principles of non-violent communication

Ten steps to peace using NVC

1 Spend some time each day quietly reflecting on how you would like to relate to yourself and others.

2 Remember that all human beings have the same needs. This helps to pay attention to the similarities between us rather than the differences.

3 Check our your intention to see if you are as interested in others getting their needs met as you getting yours met. Be honest!

4 When asking someone to do something, check first to see if you are making a request or a demand. How will you know? Here's a clue – notice what the other person's response to you is.

5 Instead of saying what you don't want someone to do, say what you do want the person to do.

6 Instead of saying what you want someone to be, say what action you'd like the person to take that you hope will help the person to be that way.

7 Before you agree or disagree with anyone's opinions, try to tune in to what that person is feeling and needing. A great way to practise is to think about the people expressing opinions on the TV or radio.

8 Instead of just saying the word 'No', say what need of yours prevents you from saying 'Yes'.

9 If you are feeling upset, think about what need of yours is not being met, and what you could do to meet it, instead of thinking about what's wrong with other people or yourself.

10 Instead of praising someone who did something you like, express your gratitude by telling the person what need of yours that action met.

The Center for Non-violent Communication (CNVC) would like there to be a critical mass of people using non-violent communication language so all people will get their needs met and resolve their conflicts peacefully.

Source: adapted from Center for Non-violent Communication (2001).

5 Transforming your anger using the five-step formula (1)

Ten steps to peace using NVC

With the drawing on the next page, imagine yourself as each of the two characters.

Write below what you imagine the 'you' on the left is thinking, feeling and needing. What kind of request might that 'you' be making in order to move to the figure on the right?

Remember you can use the feelings and needs lists to help develop your emotional vocabulary.

Do this as many times as you wish.

What is happening to me? 'v'.

What I am thinking is 'w'.

What I am feeling is 'x'.

What I am needing but not getting is 'y'.

My request (to myself or another) is 'z'.

'You 'xyz!!xx'

'Don't talk to me like that'

6 7 Steps to make ourselves angry

A Noticing Exercise

We have developed a very skilful habit of making ourselves angry.

The 7 steps of how we do it are shown below, and it happens without us moving a muscle!

Notice how often this is happening with your thoughts and then practice applying the Five Step Formula to transform your anger.

(N.B. The whole process takes about half a second to think so noticing helps to slow everything down)

STEP 1 You say or do something I don't like (or I say or do something I don't like) or you disagree with me or I disagree with me?
STEP 2 Although I may not realise it, (because I have conditioned this way), I choose to stay 'up in my head' (the path war) rather than move 'into my heart' (path of peace)
STEP 3 Although I may not realise it, I allow one or more members of 'The Should Gang' to take over my thinking, aided by the English language with its verb, to be'
STEP 4 That part of me then makes a judgement of the other person or myself, using phrases like 'I am / he is / you are.... 'rude', 'lazy', 'inconsiderate' and so on
STEP 5 Having labeled in this way, that part of me has stopped seeing you or the rest of me as a human being. It now sees you or the rest of me as a fixed object with that label.
STEP 6 It now sees itself as superior to you or the rest of me because it is telling itself that it has retained its status as a human being.
STEP 7 That part of me is then able to treat you (or I) as less than human, because that's what you or I deserve.

7 Translating unpleasant thoughts

Using the drawing on the next page, write in some of the bubbles the type of thoughts that you imagine the person is having. Then write down below how you would translate those thoughts into feelings and needs.

1 What the person is thinking is 'v'.

What I imagine they are feeling is 'w'.

What I imagine they are needing but not getting is 'x'.

2 What the person is thinking is 'v'.

What I imagine they are feeling is 'w'.

What I imagine they are needing but not getting is 'x'.

3 What the person is thinking is 'v'.

What I imagine they are feeling is 'w'.

What I imagine they are needing but not getting is 'x'.

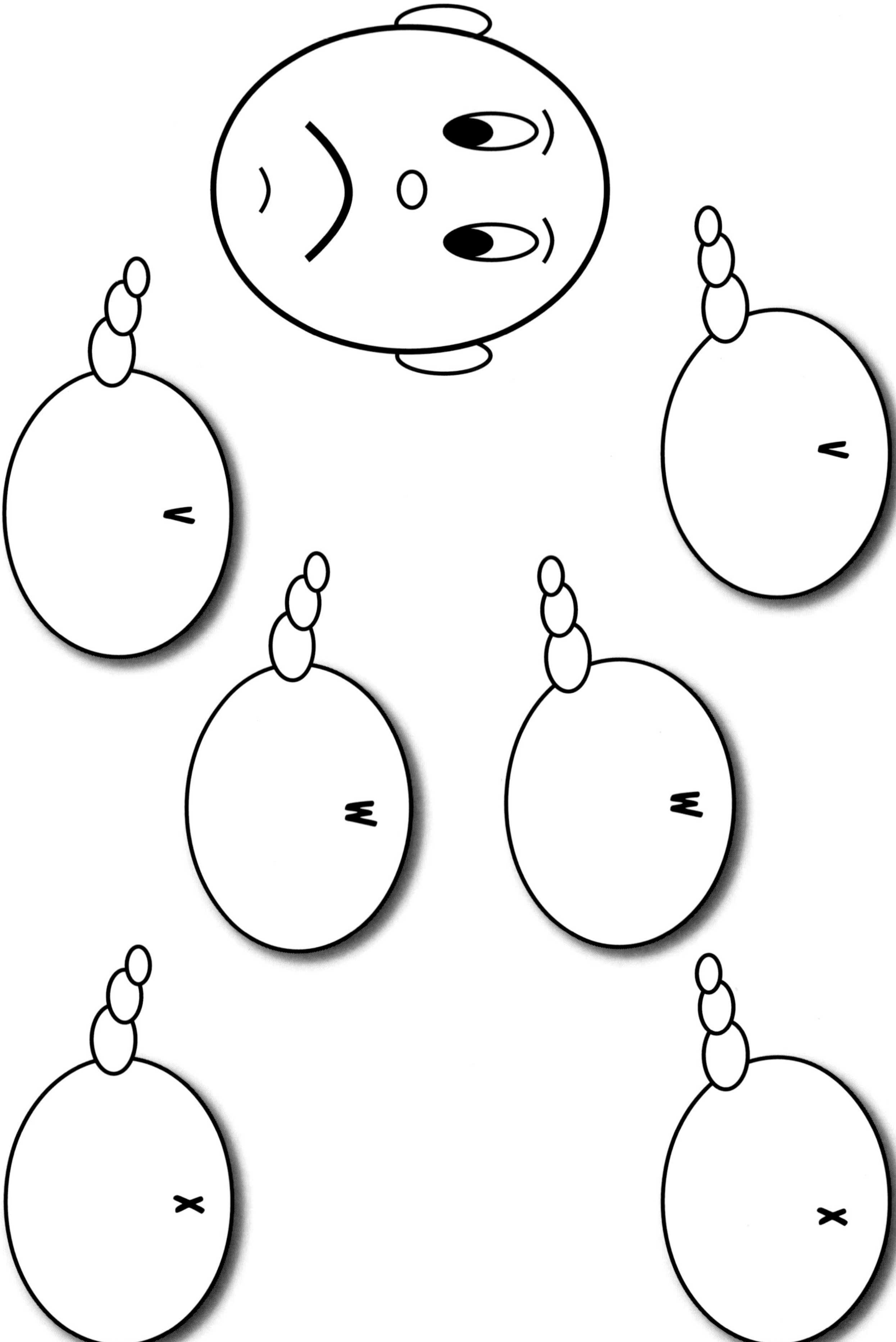
v
v
w
w
x
x

8 Translating pleasant thoughts

Using the drawing on the next page, write in some of the bubbles the type of thoughts that you imagine the person is having. Then write down below how you would translate those thoughts into feelings and needs.

1 What the person is thinking is 'v'.

What I imagine they are feeling is 'w'.

What I imagine they are needing and getting is 'x'.

2 What the person is thinking is 'v'.

What I imagine they are feeling is 'w'.

What I imagine they are needing and getting is 'x'.

3 What the person is thinking is 'v'.

What I imagine they are feeling is 'w'.

What I imagine they are needing and getting is 'x'.

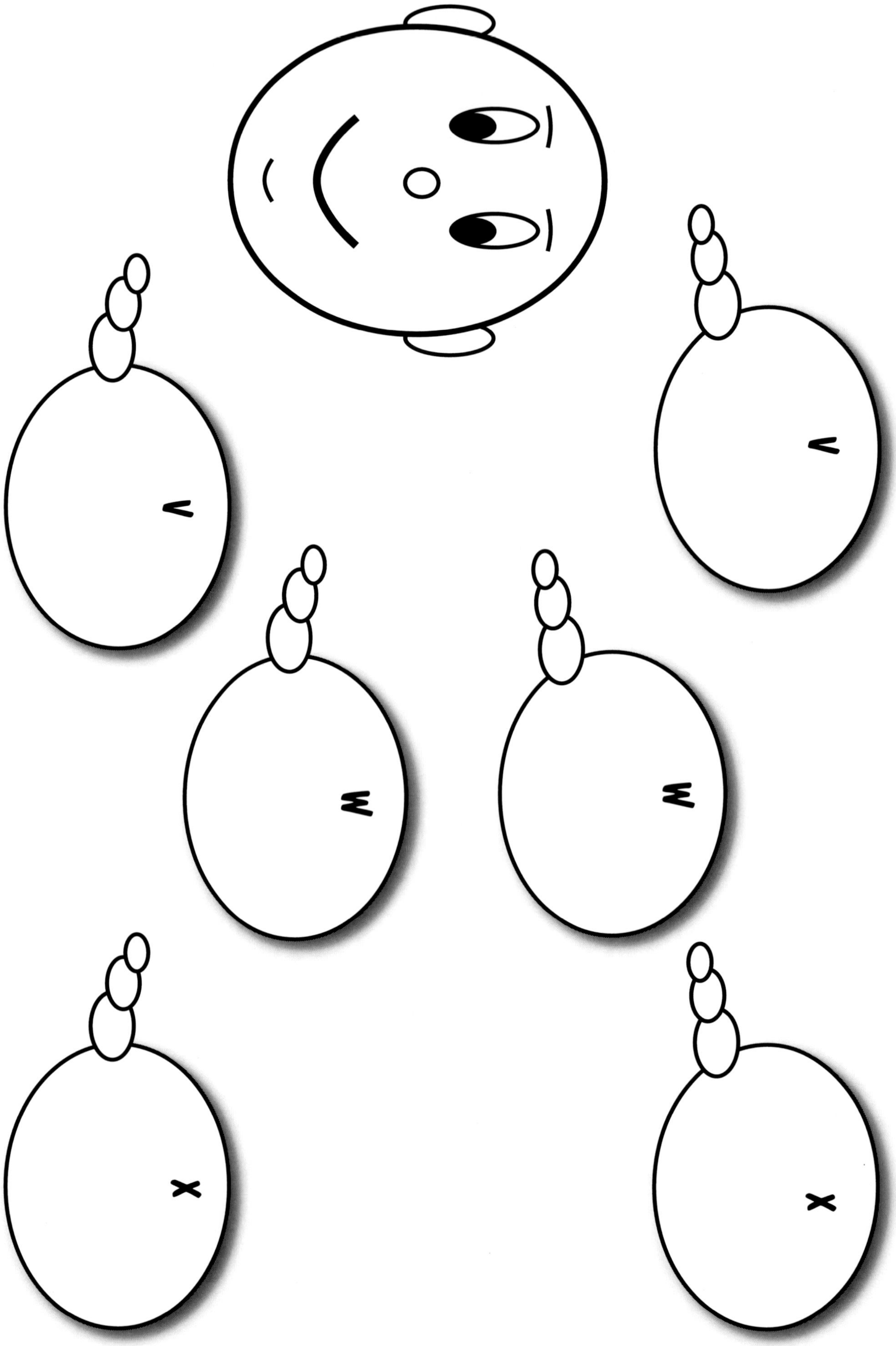

9 Transforming attacks from the 'should gang'

Here is some practice that you can do when you are in a queue for a bus, a train, in a shop or suchlike. Just look casually at the people around you for a few minutes.

Start to notice what thoughts are going through your mind. Make a point of remembering some of these thoughts and then write out a few of them below.

Do you notice any that are judgements of others? Remember, these are thoughts that have been created by the 'should gang'.

Now is a good time to translate some of those thoughts into your feelings, needs and requests.

What I was thinking was …

Translation:

I was feeling 'x'

because I was needing 'y'

and my request is 'z'.

What I was thinking was …

Translation:

I was feeling 'x'

because I was needing 'y'

and my request is 'z'.

10 Passive, aggressive or assertive – what's the difference?

These activities provide you with the chance to find out which of the three approaches you typically use to respond to people and situations, and how to use the five-step formula to improve your communication.

Aggressive behaviour

Typically, your behaviour is described as aggressive when:

- You put people down.
- You want your own way at any cost.
- You treat others in ways that you would not like and justify it with such thoughts as: 'It doesn't matter', or 'They deserved it for what they did to me or one of my friends or family.'
- You use your power to get others to do what you want, even if they do not want to.

Can you remember when you have behaved like this? Choose one specific event, apply the five-step formula and write out your responses below.

Step 1: What actually happened?

Step 2: What was I thinking? (Shall I translate that into feelings and needs before I say any of it out loud?)

Step 3: What was I feeling?

Step 4: What was I needing but not getting?

Step 5: If I had my time over again, the request I would make to myself or the other person would be ....

Your turn:

Passive behaviour

Typically, your behaviour is described as passive when:

- You apologise frequently.
- You say 'yes' when you want to say 'no'.
- You sulk, hint or sigh frequently.
- You do nothing or avoid people and situations that you imagine will be difficult.
- You hope others will guess what you want or need.
- You agree to do something you have no time for or do not want to do.

Can you remember when you have behaved like this? Choose one specific event, apply the five-step formula and write out your responses below.

Step 1: What actually happened?

Step 2: What was I thinking? (Shall I translate that into feelings and needs before I say anything out loud?)

Step 3: What was I feeling?

Step 4: What was I needing but not getting?

Step 5: If I had my time over again, the request I would make to myself or the other person would be ....

Your turn:

Assertive behaviour

Typically, your behaviour is described as assertive when:

- You listen carefully to others.
- You are clear about and are actually saying what you are thinking and feeling.
- You think of others and are willing to ask them how they feel.
- You ask confidently for what you want.
- You take responsibility for both your behaviour and your choices.
- You are not concerned about people thinking that you are a 'good' or 'nice' person.
- You think well of yourself and others.
- You acknowledge your rights and those of others.

Can you remember when you have behaved like this? Choose one specific event, apply the five-step formula and write out your responses below.

In this example, question 4 asks what you were needing and getting, rather than not getting.

Step 1: What actually happened?

Step 2: What was I thinking? (Shall I translate that into feelings and needs before I say anything out loud?)

Step 3: What was I feeling?

Step 4: What was I needing and getting?

Step 5: If I had my time over again, the request I would make to myself or the other person would be ....

Your turn:

11 Drama triangle questions and answers

Remember a situation where you were involved in a drama triangle. Notice which role you had to start with. Were you the rescuer, victim or persecutor? Did you notice any change in your role as the drama developed?

With that situation in mind, read through the list of questions below and choose at least six that interest you. Write out your chosen questions and your answers to them in the space below the list.

1 What was I not doing?
2 What did I need to do?
3 Who was taking responsibility for whom?
4 Who was I taking responsibility for?
5 Was I allowing the other person to take responsibility for themselves and their actions?
6 Who had the power in the situation and what makes me say that?
7 Had I agreed to do more than I wanted to do?
8 Was I doing more than my fair share and how did I know that to be true?
9 How powerful did I feel?
10 Was I using my power to set my own boundaries and take responsibility for my actions?
11 What boundaries did I need to set up and how could I have done this?
12 Was I using my power to take care of myself properly?
13 What was I feeling about this situation?
14 What would I have liked to feel?
15 Was there anything I needed and wasn't getting?
16 What request did I need to make so that everybody won?

Your chosen questions and your answers:

12 Red rags and how not to be a bull

This is an activity for identifying people, things and/or situations that irritate, frustrate or anger you, how you typically respond and how to change that into an authentic response.

Example Situation: Cups that need to be washed are frequently left in the sink at the end of the day.

Typical response	Rarely	Sometimes	Frequently
Nagging	X	X	✓
Shouting	X	X	✓

Typical response: 'I'm fed up with you being so inconsiderate and thoughtless. Every morning I come down and have to clean up after you. I'm not your slave, you know. It's time you stopped being so lazy.'

Apply five-step formula:

Step 1: What has happened or is happening?

Step 2: What are you thinking? (Ask yourself whether it is more helpful to translate this silently into feelings and needs before you say anything.)

Step 3: What was I feeling?

Step 4: What was I needing but not getting?

Step 5: What request am I making of others or myself in a do-able form that aims to get my needs met?

Five-step formula response:
'When I see cups in the sink I feel irritated because I'd like help to keep the kitchen tidy. Would you be willing to wash the cups and put them away when you've finished with them?'

Write examples here of people, things and/or situations which irritate, frustrate or anger you.

-
-
-
-

Now fill in the sheet opposite to identify your typical response to one of the above and tick under the most accurate heading.

Situation:

Typical response	Rarely	Sometimes	Frequently
Nagging			
Shouting			
Interrupting			
Exploding			
Threatening			
Correcting			
Insulting			
Sarcasm			
Revenge			
Withdrawal			
Sulking			
Taking it out on someone else			
Ignoring the problem			
Feeling ill			
Feeling depressed			
Being polite but feeling angry under the surface			
Other responses not listed			

Write out your typical response below and then translate that into a five-step formula response.

Typical response:
Five-step formula response:

You can repeat this exercise with other situations from your list.

13 Phrases for summarising and finding ways forward

Summarising phrases

I have found this first set of phrases to be useful when I'm in dialogue with someone and want them to know that I'm hearing what they're saying en route to finding a win–win outcome.

Remembering the chapter on NLP, notice how many of the five senses are covered by these phrases.

'Before we go on'

'Can I just check I heard you right?'
'Can I just run over that again with you?'
'Can you explain what you meant by...?'
'So from what you've just said, I understand...'.
'So to pull all these strands together, what you're saying is...'
'So just to make sure we're on the same wavelength...'
'So what you're telling me is...'
'So what I've just picked up from what you're saying is...'
'What I hear you saying is...'.

Finding ways forward phrases

I choose from this next set of phrases when seeking to move a situation forward. They fit into the request stage of the five-step formula.

'So what would you like to happen next?'
'What could you do to sort this out?'
'How could you improve the way things are for you?'
'How do you really want things to be?'
'What would you really like to see happen here?'
'Apart from that?'
'If it wasn't like that, how might it be?'
'If a wise person were here now, what might they suggest?'
'If you stepped into your future, how might it be there?'
'If you had a magic wand, what might you wish for? And what would that do for you?'

14 Changing your anger in your private cinema

Imagine yourself owning your own private cinema and sitting in your very comfortable seat. You've had a film made of what's making you angry.

Start the film.

Notice who you're with, where you are, how you're dressed, how you're standing or sitting. Listen to what's being said, and what you're saying and how you're saying it.

You can stop the scene at any time and make any changes to what you're saying and doing.

Note: You can only make changes to what *you* are saying or doing.

Run this changed scene.

Now step into the scene so that *you* are looking out through your own eyes. See what you see, hear what you hear and feel how good this feels.

If you want to make any further changes to what you are doing or saying in the scene, sit back down in your comfy seat and make those changes.

Again, step into the scene and notice what it is like now.

Close your eyes and imagine future situations where you can behave in the way that you have just created. See what you see, hear what you hear and feel how good this new way of behaving feels.

Enjoy!

15 Changing your image of anger

Allow yourself to feel your anger.

Notice where in your body it's living.

Imagine it as a firework with a really long fuse, or as a stick of dynamite, like in a cartoon. See the fuse alight and sparkling and starting its journey towards an explosion.

Make the colour of the flame big, bright and colourful. Now make the flame travel more slowly. And slower still. Make the colour start to drain away so that it becomes a black and white image.

Make the fuse get smaller.

Smaller still.

Make the whole image a black and white photo.

Take the very small photo and tear it up into little pieces. Drop the pieces in the bin. Take three deep breaths.

Smile.

What do you notice about how you are feeling now?

16 Change from feeling angry to feeling great

Think about someone who annoys, irritates or intimidates you.

Close your eyes and make an image of them. Have them look at you in whatever way they do when they trouble you.

Hear them say whatever they say and notice the tone, pitch and speed of their voice. Remember the way they are standing or sitting and any gestures they make or what movements they make. Really bring the image to life.

Now take the image and change it from colour to black and white. If it was like a film, make it a still image like a photograph.

Now move the image from where you are holding it in your mind's eye to a place far off in the distance. Make it much smaller, at most an eighth of the size. Place a clown's red nose on the person.

Hear them say what they say, but change their voice so that it sounds like a cartoon character you find amusing, such as Bart Simpson.

Notice how you are feeling in relation to them and what they have done or said in the past now that you have control of where and how they live inside you. Feel free to play with further changes you want to make. Find out what works best and use that until there is little or no emotional charge left for you.

17 How to feel wonderful

Remember a time when you felt wonderful.

Close your eyes and remember that time in vivid detail. Allow yourself to see those images clearly, hear the sounds loudly and remember the feelings just as they were back then.

If you are not already in it, step into that experience now and imagine yourself being in that memory as if it were happening right now. See what you see, hear what you hear and feel how good it feels to be in it again. Make the colours stronger and brighter if that helps, and take a moment to remember how you were breathing back then. Breathe like that again now.

Notice where in your body you are feeling wonderful right now. Get a sense of where the feeling starts, where it goes and in which direction the feeling is moving. Up or down, side to side, round in a circle? Imagine taking control of this feeling and its movement and spinning it faster and faster and stronger and stronger throughout your body as the feelings increase.

Imagine a time in the future when you could use these feelings to good effect. Spin the feelings throughout your body as you think about the next few weeks or about anything special coming up where you imagine it will be great to feel these wonderful feelings. Do not be at all surprised if you feel wonderful for absolutely no reason at all.

18 How to change a troubling image of someone

To make this technique work best, you will need to do it on your own standing up and with enough space to move into one of the four different positions outlined below.

This is a rapid and effective way of changing your perception of others' behaviour so that it no longer bothers you.

The four positions

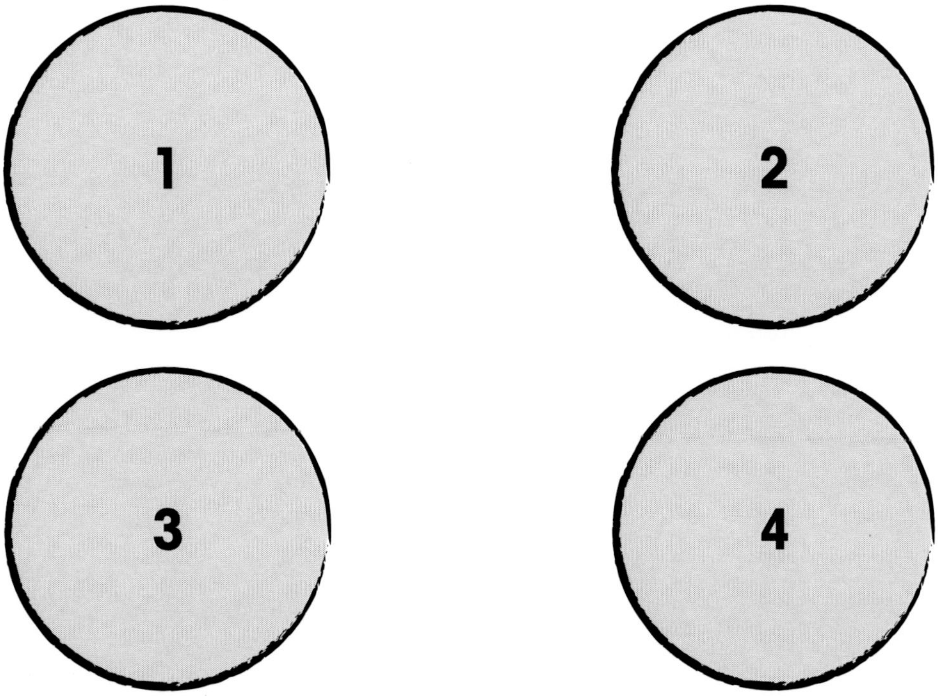

Here's how to do this technique

1 Mark out four positions that you can move into easily in your chosen undisturbed space.

2 Stand in position 1 facing the person whose behaviour you are not enjoying. Imagine that they are standing in position 2.

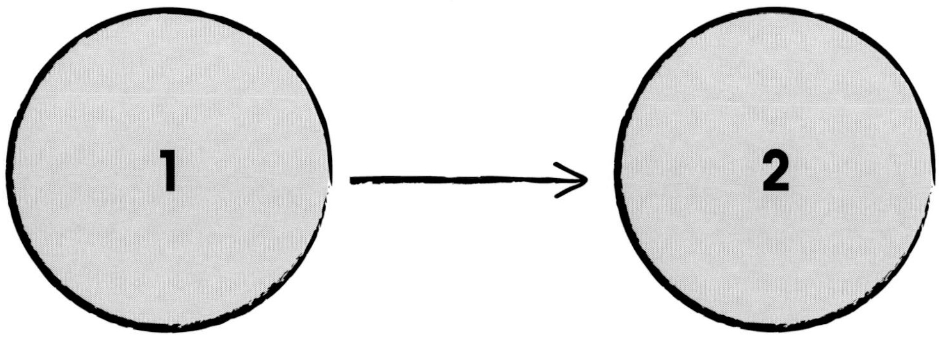

3 As you face the person, ask yourself what you are experiencing in your body, and what you are thinking and feeling.

4 Step away from position 1 and think about something different and mundane for a moment, for example, what you ate for your last meal.

5 Step into position 2 as if you were the other person and look at position 1.

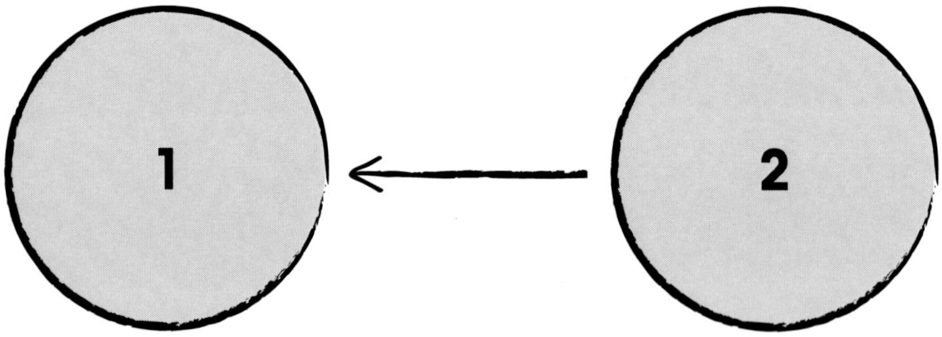

6 As in step 3 above, notice what you are experiencing in your body, and what you are thinking and feeling.

7 As before, think about something else, for example, what your favourite colour is.

8 Now step into position 3, look across at position 1 and ask, 'How do you here, in position 3, respond to that you there, in position 1? Are there any resources that you need?' Speak out loud whatever comes to your mind.

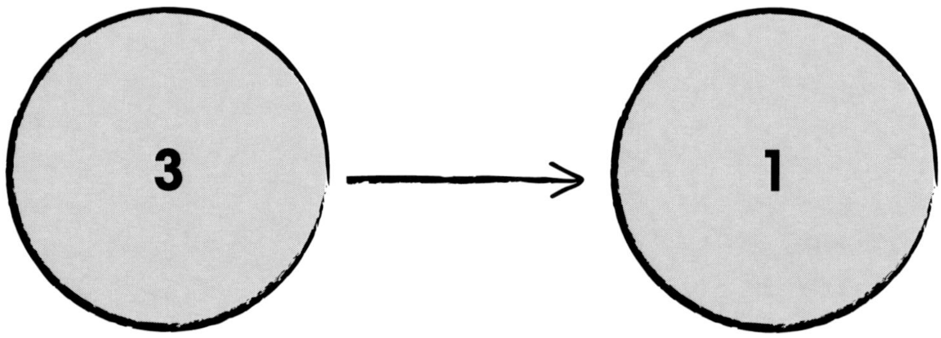

9 Now step into position 4 and, with arms out straight, point your index fingers at positions 1 and 3. Raising your arms, lift up and out and swap over what was in those previous positions. Your arms will now be crossed.

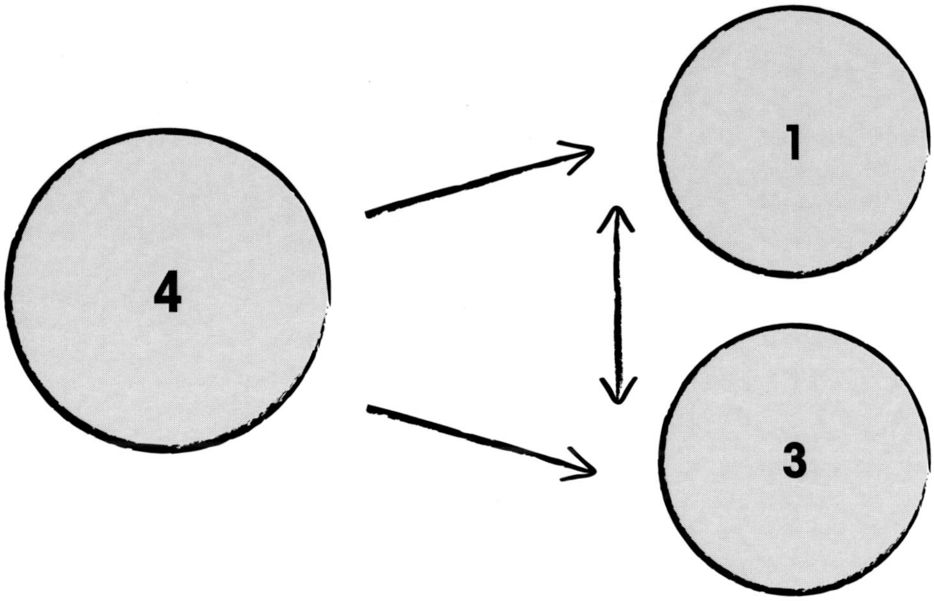

10 Go back to position 1 and look across at position 2 where you once again imagine the other person to be.

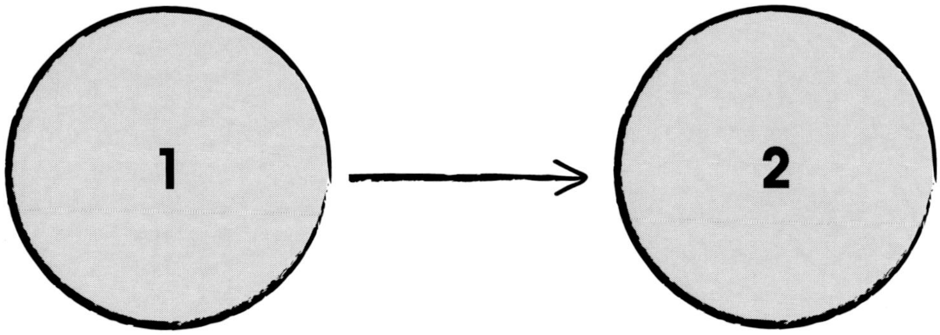

11 Notice now what you are experiencing and ask yourself, 'How is this different now?'

12 Now step into position 2 as if you were the other person, look across to position 1 and ask the same question.

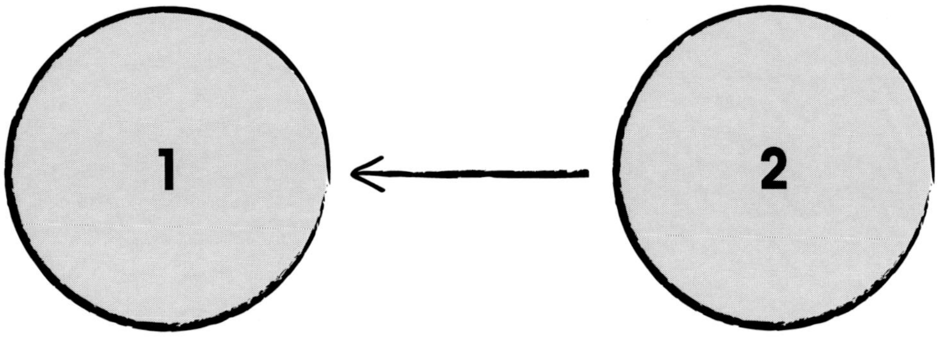

13 Finally, step back to position 1 and allow yourself to come home to yourself.

Notice whether you are feeling and thinking any differently about the other person compared with how you were at the start. Has anything occurred to you to do differently in the future with this person? If not, just notice whether anything just 'drops in' over the next day or so.

19 How to use the EFT cooling tower technique

Think of a problem in your life that is causing you to be 'at war' with somebody, or something in your life that you are 'heated up' about.

Use a 'heat-ometer' to measure the intensity of your feelings about the situation on a scale of 0 to 10.

Close your eyes and allow yourself to focus on the scene in your mind's eye. Imagine what you want to do to get revenge. Make this as graphic as you wish. Imagine saying what you really want to say.

Using the tapping explanation in Chapter 2, do a round of tapping while imagining you are sending all the thoughts, words and images up through your head as though you were releasing steam through a chimney.

Keep doing rounds of tapping until all the images have evaporated like steam and you have zero intensity of feeling on your 'heat-ometer'.

20 Using EFT in an argument

This is a very helpful technique when one or more people are expressing anger and the normal method of tapping would prove difficult.

As soon as you sense someone being angry with you, begin to gently tap together the thumb and little finger of your left hand.

As you look at the person who is angry with you, keep tapping and saying to yourself phrases such as:

- Even though x is angry with me, I like myself.
- Even though I don't know why x is acting this way, I respect myself.
- Even though x is trying to goad me, I really like the way I'm dealing with this situation.
- Even though I may be causing x a problem, I still accept myself.

This also works if you are feeling angry with someone else. Do exactly the same with your thumb and little finger, only this time use variations of the phrases above in this way:

- Even though I'm angry at x, I like myself.
- Even though I don't know why I'm acting this way with x, I respect myself.
- And so on.

Believe it or not, you can simultaneously speak to the other person, tap and run these phrases through your mind. Don't take my word for it, though – try it yourself.

21 Feel differently with a guided visualisation

The trouble tree and the secret garden

Imagine yourself out in the countryside. A place of peace and calm. Trees, open fields, rolling hills, fragrance in the air, bright sun warming your body, the easy sound of birds up above…

There is a path that beckons you, so you take smooth, steady steps along its gentle surface. You are in no rush and are pleased to be able to take your time as you allow in all the sights, sounds and aromas that surround you on this magical day.

Up ahead you notice a tree with many branches, some which reach quite low, making them very easy to touch.

You notice a sign at the foot of the tree – you know the sort of sign, telling you what the tree is called in English and Latin.

You look a little closer, for you are curious, never having seen a tree quite like this before. You do a 'double take', because the tree is called 'Your Trouble Tree' and you notice some instructions written out beneath:

'This tree asks you to hang up all your troubles on its many branches so that you can continue on your walk trouble free. No worry too small.'

You stop, feeling a bit amused and a bit silly. You look around.

No one is in sight. So you think 'Why not?' and allow yourself to be aware of the worries that are alive in you at this time. Maybe it's to do with money, work, family, friends, or something else.

And now let yourself imagine attaching each worry to a branch of your very own trouble tree. They'll be kept safe for you to collect at the end of your walk.

You finish and decide to walk on along the path, which rises gently ahead of you. The air is still warm, the sun is bright and soothing to your skin. The scents delight you as you stroll along. And you notice a small, wooden gate up ahead, just to the side of the path. As you get closer, you notice that this too has a small sign on it. It says 'My Secret Garden'.

With the same kind of mixture of delight and self-consciousness that you had back at your trouble tree, you look around to see if anyone else is in sight. No one. You peer over the gate and see the most beautiful country garden, totally sheltered by a hedge running all the way round it.

You open the gate, walk into the garden, close the gate behind you and just stand there for a moment, taking everything in. You notice the colours of the flowers and plants. You bend down carefully to smell the sweet fragrances and you can hear the joyful birdsong and feel the soft grass beneath your feet. You have a real sense of peace and calm.

You notice a wooden bench ahead of you and you decide to rest there, letting your eyes close, just absorbing all of the sweetness and joy that surround you right now.

You notice the easy rise and fall of your breath, letting it slow and deepen as you sit there in comfort, being nourished with every breath, from the outside in, allowing that nourishment to find its way into every part of you, every cell, every atom and molecule of you.

You have a deep sense of peace here, so you decide to rest a while.

And then, as you breathe out, you open your eyes, and slowly stretch and quietly let your senses take in the richness of your own special place, knowing that it is yours to visit at any time.

You calmly get to your feet, and with a deep breath, take a small step towards the gate. With a last look for now, you close the gate behind you and make your way back down the path.

You take in the rolling hills, the waving patterns in the grass as the breeze dances playfully, the clear sky and the warming sun on your body. It feels good to be alive.

And arriving back at your trouble tree, you might want to take some of your troubles back, or you may decide to leave them there for safe keeping. It's what the tree's there for, after all.

Or you may notice that in taking any of them back, they may be a different size or shape or weight. You can choose. And you can choose to revisit any or all of this at any time you wish: perhaps when you're on your journey home as a passenger in a car, on a bus or train, or last thing at night before falling into sleep.

Feel free to choose.

22 Visualisation for healing anger

First of all, get in touch with where in your body your anger is living – is it in your head, neck, shoulders, stomach or more than one place?

Once you've done that, imagine you are going to journey inside your body, like the submarine in the film *Fantastic Voyage* that gets shrunk to tiny proportions and injected into a human body. Imagine you're inside that submarine looking out of its windows.

See the muscles, bones, tendons and ligaments. Now go inside the part where you feel your anger most. See the cells around you, and go inside one of the cells. See the proteins, the enzymes and the DNA. Go inside one of the strands of DNA and notice the atoms it's made from. Choose one of the atoms and move inside.

As you do this, you and your submarine continue to shrink to infinitesimally small dimensions which allow you to see the minute particles that make up an atom – the protons, electrons and neutrons, all moving freely around. And last of all, enter the quantum field itself, the source of these sub-atomic particles, the very source of life itself. Here is held all possibility, all creation.

Perhaps you imagine it like a lake or as deep dark space with nothing in it, or as a faint hum, like the breath of a sleeping animal, waiting to be woken. And see and feel what sort of disturbance the anger in your body is making to the deep dark space or to the steady hum. In your mind, ask to be shown if it's not obvious. Are there waves and ripples on that lake or in that space? Are the sounds erratic, discordant, grating or screeching?

And once you have a strong image of how the anger is disturbing the source inside you, say firmly in your mind the word 'cancel'. Notice how the disturbance stops and everything settles into a more peaceful and steady order.

Now imagine yourself with a small stone of a colour of your choice. Let the stone represent a quality that you wish to manifest in that part of you that was disturbed previously by your anger. It might be peace, or compassion or forgiveness. You choose. Let the stone drop and fall into the lake, the space or the hum with your chosen quality clearly in your mind as you do so.

Notice how the stone changes everything for the better.

The lake or space may have become the same colour as your stone, or the hum may have changed to an even more appealing sound. You can choose more than one quality if you so wish.

You have now replaced the disturbance of anger with something much more appealing. And now move from that place of creation to the sub-atomic level and, in your mind, say the words 'Show me it is done' to bring that change with you. Notice what's different.

Now move back up to the atoms themselves, and again say in your mind 'Show me it is done', and notice what has changed. Perhaps the atoms themselves have taken on the colour of your stone(s). Now back up to the DNA with the same request, up to the cells, the body part where you most noticed the anger originally, making the same request, 'Show me that it is done', and noticing what is different.

And last, as you come out of your whole body, say in your mind, or out loud if you wish, 'It is done, it is done, it is done.'

Take a few deep breaths – and it is indeed, done!

23 What makes me angry?

Identify your anger triggers by keeping a diary or log for a week or so.

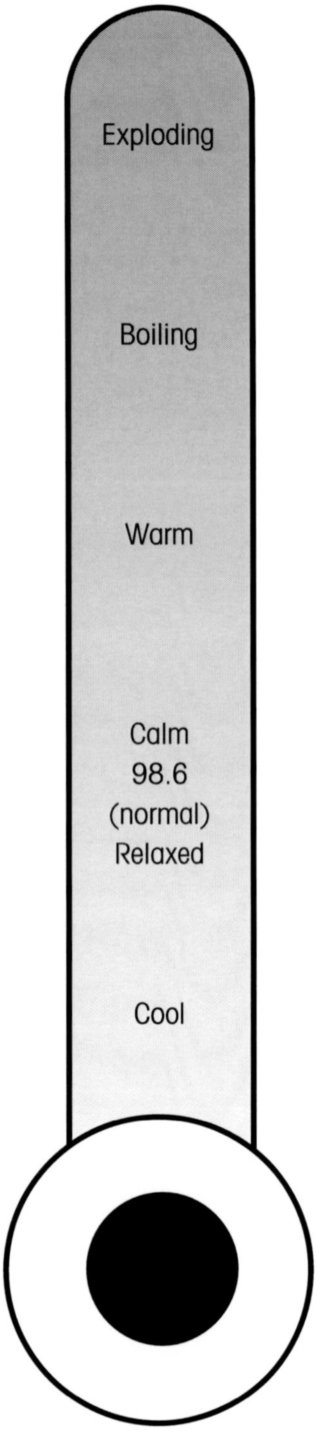

What makes me angry:

Source: Faupel *et al,* 1998, p60

24 How do I feel when I start to get angry?

Think about how you feel when you first start to get angry. Tick any of the following statements that apply to you.

I feel hot.

My hands start to sweat.

I find it difficult to stay still; I get fidgety.

My mouth gets dry.

My hands go into fists.

My body feels tense.

My heart races.

I breathe more quickly.

I feel panicky.

Describe three other things that you have noticed about yourself when you are beginning to get angry:

1
2
3

Source: Faupel *et al*, 1998, p92

25 Volcano in your tummy?

Do you have a volcano in your tummy or explosions in your head?

When we feel angry, things happen to our bodies. Draw what happens to you. Label your picture, for example, red face.

Source: Whitehouse & Pudney, 1996, p21

26 Bottling anger

Write in the spaces the anger you may have bottled up. Who? When? Where? Why?

Source: Whitehouse & Pudney, 1996, p23

27 Are you a volcano?

Print words on the flame of the volcano to show what happens during an explosion of anger. Print words on the lava flow to show what damage can result.

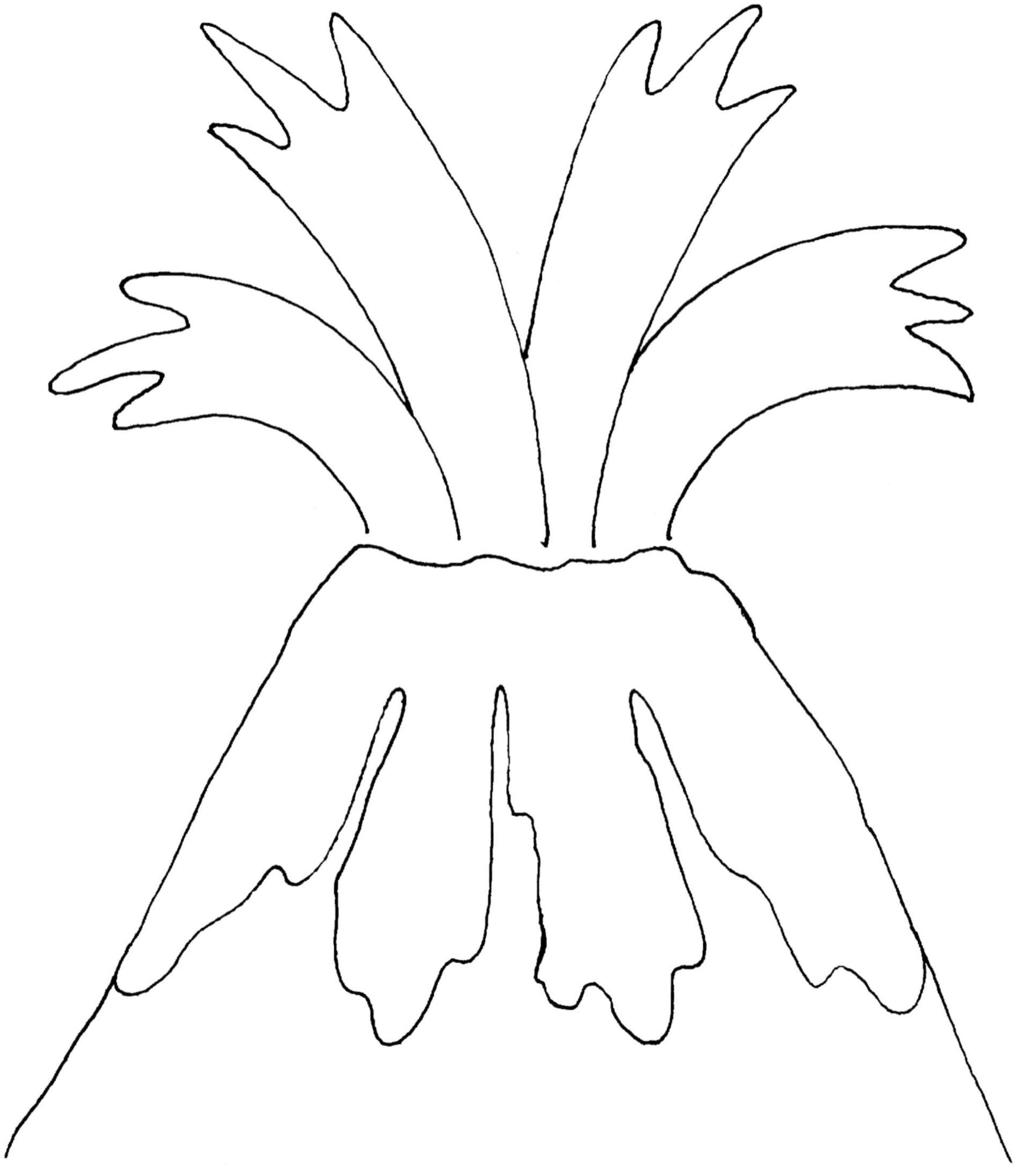

Source: Whitehouse & Pudney, 1996, p25

28 Time out

What could you do to calm down and keep out of trouble? Go through the Time Out doors and fill in the spaces with your ideas.

Source: Whitehouse & Pudney, 1996, p39

29 Keeping calm

Dampening the fuse!

Here is a list of things that some people do in order to help them calm down when they recognise the feelings that go along with being angry.

Choose three that you think might work for you and add any of your own that you have thought of or tried.

1 Walking away from the incident.
2 Counting to ten.
3 Talking yourself into feeling calm.
4 Using a catchphrase.
5 Pretending to be somewhere else.
6 Hiding behind an imaginary shield.
7 Using the turtle technique and protecting yourself inside your shell.
8 Taking some exercise – running, football, shooting baskets.
9 Having a special place to go.
10 Having a special person to be with.
11 Listening to music.
12 Breathing deeply and slowly.
13 Relaxing clenched muscles.

The three that I think I will try are:

Other things that I do to help me stay calm are:

Source: adapted from Faupel *et al,* 1998.

30 What do you do when you want to swear?

A lot of people swear when they want to let their anger out. Sometimes it's a quick way of letting out angry feelings, sometimes people swear because they can't think of all the words to express what they are feeling, sometimes they use the swear words they hear from their family or their friends.

A lot of people don't like to hear other people swearing. Parents or teachers might think, 'People will think I'm a bad parent (or teacher) if I let my children swear.' Others don't like to hear 'God' used for swearing.

A lot of swear words are about parts of our bodies and things we do with our bodies. Some people feel uncomfortable with these words. Whatever the reason, swearing can get you into trouble.

One alternative could be to make up your own swear words that won't offend anyone. Can you think of some?

Source: Whitehouse & Pudney, 1996, p71

31 Word search (1)

S	G	T	M	C	R	Y	G	D	N	A	R
H	L	A	U	G	H	Z	M	Q	T	W	M
O	S	D	E	E	E	B	Q	H	R	E	M
U	O	E	I	V	O	L	G	W	X	U	C
T	J	R	I	O	E	I	C	U	G	U	I
Y	P	P	J	L	F	T	E	X	P	S	A
F	Q	M	H	A	F	R	A	I	D	U	K
P	P	A	P	A	Z	Y	M	H	U	G	C
Z	W	T	G	N	T	Q	R	K	H	D	T
L	J	S	W	G	R	E	W	F	I	F	D
U	M	O	G	R	P	C	S	A	T	H	S
B	H	P	Y	Y	U	Z	V	A	O	J	K
M	A	R	O	H	A	X	T	R	X	B	J

Find the following words in the maze above. They may go up, down, across or diagonally.

Afraid	**Angry**	**Fight**	**Shout**
Stamp	**Laugh**	**Cry**	**Red**
Hate	**Love**	**Hug**	**Hit**

32 Word search (2)

F	O	R	G	I	V	E	X	P	R	E	S	S
E	L	P	U	C	E	T	R	O	P	P	U	S
E	M	E	M	A	S	B	O	O	K	U	A	I
L	A	D	F	R	I	G	H	T	E	N	E	D
I	V	O	S	I	X	W	S	E	N	C	O	P
N	A	L	A	N	C	X	E	E	S	H	Z	U
G	Y	P	R	G	D	I	S	T	R	U	S	T
S	L	X	C	E	R	U	T	T	T	A	U	D
I	E	E	A	L	B	D	H	T	R	F	L	O
E	N	B	S	A	B	I	H	T	U	E	K	W
C	O	M	M	U	N	I	C	A	T	I	O	N
H	L	O	O	K	E	N	A	S	H	V	R	S
S	H	O	N	E	S	T	C	K	C	A	R	B

1 Find these words in the maze above. They may go up, down, across or diagonally.

Frightened	Forgive	Sulk	Ask	Truth
Explode	Sarcasm	Feelings	Express	Communication
Distrust	Think	Abuse	Support	Lonely
Punch	Caring	Putdown	Honest	

2 Divide the words into two lists: 'Healthy' communication, 'Damaging' communication

Source: Whitehouse & Pudney, 1996, p67

33 Crossword

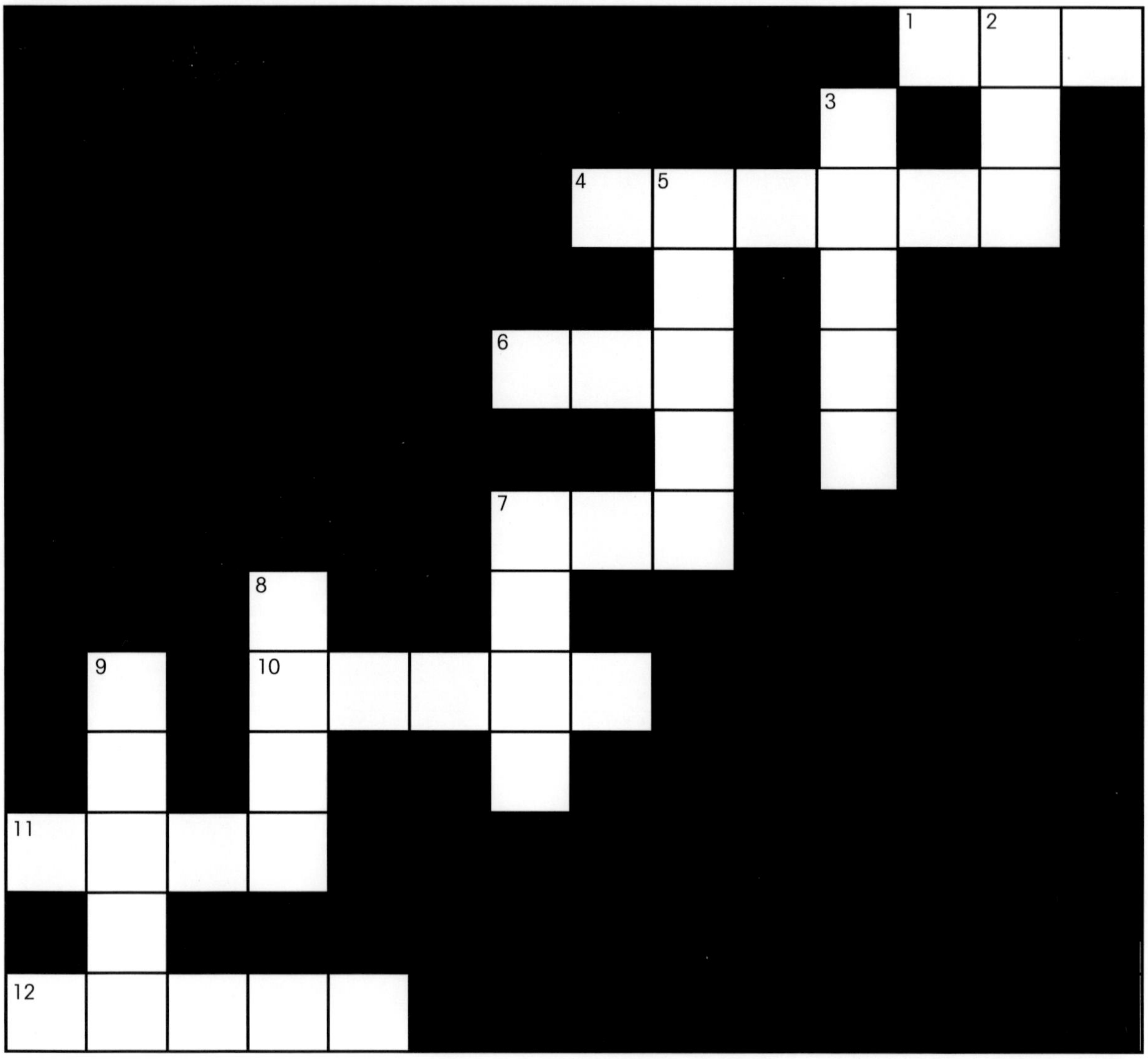

Across clues

1 When I feel sad I …

4 I am … of lions and tigers.

6 A … makes me feel good.

7 Don't …, it hurts.

10 When someone teases me I feel …

11 I … my cat.

12 When I am angry I could … my feet.

Down clues

2 John got angry and his face went …

3 When I feel happy I …

5 If people … someone might get hurt.

7 If I get hit it will …

8 I … people who hurt me.

9 When I get angry I …

Source: Whitehouse & Pudney, 1996, p68.

34 Solutions to word searches and crossword

Word search (1)

Word	Row	Column	Direction
Afraid	7	5	E
Angry	8	5	S
Fight	6	6	NE
Shout	1	1	S
Stamp	10	3	N
Laugh	2	2	E
Hate	8	9	NW
Love	6	5	N
Hug	8	9	E
Hit	9	10	S
Cry	1	5	E
Red	5	3	N

Word search (2)

Word	Row	Column	Direction
Frightened	4	4	E
Truth	8	10	S
Support	2	13	W
Forgive	1	1	E
Explode	9	3	N
Lonely	12	2	N
Sulk	7	12	S
Sarcasm	5	4	S
Punch	2	11	S
Ask	11	9	S
Feelings	1	1	S
Caring	2	5	S
Communication	11	1	E
Express	1	7	E
Putdown	5	13	S
Distrust	7	6	E
Abuse	10	5	NE
Honest	13	2	E
Think	8	9	SW

Crossword

Across	**Down**
1 cry	2 red
4 afraid	3 laugh
6 hug	5 fight
7 hit	7 hurt
10 angry	8 hate
11 love	9 shout
12 stamp	

Source: Whitehouse & Pudney, 1996, p69.

35 A heartfelt letter from your child

Dear Mum and Dad,

Please help me to love myself. Don't spoil me. I know quite well that I shouldn't have all that I ask for. I'm only testing you. Please show me the discipline that I need.

And allow me my sense of dignity, so please don't belittle me in front of other people. I'll take a whole lot more notice if you talk to me with as much respect as you give your best grown-up friend.

Don't ridicule me or imply that my behaviour means I am a bad person. This will just erode my sense of worthiness.

Don't be too upset when sometimes I say 'I hate you'. It's not you I hate but your power over me.

Please don't shout or nag. If you do, I shall have to protect myself by pretending to be deaf.

Please be patient with me the way that you are with a fragile plant that has a long growing season.

And if you've had a bad day yourself, can you not take it out on me?

Please help me feel good about myself by telling me of all the good things about myself more often than you tell me of the things that you don't like.

Don't bribe me or make rash promises. Remember that I feel badly let down when promises are broken.

The more you give me the safety to expose my true feelings, the more of my inner beauty I will risk showing.

Please be as consistent as you can be. When you're not, I get very confused and it really makes it hard to have faith in you.

Please accept my fears as real: I hate it when you tell me not to be silly.

You may be surprised to know that when you say sorry after you've made a mistake, you go up in my esteem. This lets me know that mistakes are OK and I can say sorry to you too.

Please keep on praising me and acknowledging me for who I am, not for what I do. That allows me to grow up without the stress of competing with and comparing myself with others in the family.

Nearly lastly, please remember that I thrive with a lot of love and understanding.

Totally lastly, always remember that I love you and I don't expect you to be perfect either. That way we can all get along a whole lot better.

And thank you. Thank you for being you and for bringing me into the world to take my place and play my part.

With love,

Your child

36 Improving the way I feel about myself

Use the drawings on the next two pages as a template to think about and write out those characteristics and qualities that you like about yourself.

What do you do well now, or what have you done well in the past?

Do colour the drawings in or embellish them with more than just words. Put them in a prominent place and make a commitment to look at them each day for the next 21 days.

My Good Qualities

37 The rubber band of change

I agree that it takes 21 days of continuous practice to change a habit.

To make it easy to make any changes, try this technique:

- Find a rubber band that fits comfortably around your wrist.
- Notice when you are being 'attacked' by the judgemental thoughts of the 'should gang'. (You'll recognise them by the number of 'shoulds', 'oughts', 'have tos' and 'musts' you'll be thinking, as well as the harshness of their tone.)
- Either touch or turn the band if it's easy to do, then take the band from the wrist you are wearing it on and put it on the other one.
- After doing this easily and consistently, ask yourself what feelings and needs of yours are under the words of judgement that the 'should gang' are using on you. For example, if you are calling yourself 'lazy', a way to 'translate' into feelings and needs might be this way: 'Am I feeling upset at my lack of progress or motivation?'
- After getting into this habit, add this last piece.

As well as translating the judgemental thoughts and words of the 'should gang' into feelings and needs, replace any of those thoughts with another thought. This time, make it one of gratitude or appreciation for one specific aspect of your life. It can be the area where you live, a person in your life, an item of food that you enjoy, a piece of music, the blue sky or the rain. It really doesn't matter as long as you give yourself just a few moments to connect fully with the thought and any feelings that surface in you as a result.

References

Bandler R (2008) *Get the Life You Want,* Harper Element, London.

Berne E (1964) *Games People Play,* Grove Press, New York.

Bly R, Hillman J & Meade M (eds) (1993) *The Rag and Bone Shop of the Heart: Poems for Men,* Harper Perennial, London.

Casey K (2006) *Each Day a New Beginning: Daily Meditations for Women,* Hazelden Foundation, Center City, MN.

Center for Non-violent Communication (2001, revised 2004 by Gary Baran and CNVC), *10 things we can do to contribute to internal, interpersonal, and organizational peace,* online, www.cnvc.org/en/Training/10-steps-peace (accessed August 2010).

Center for Non-violent Communication (2005a) *Feelings inventory, online,* www.cnvc.org/en/Training/feelings-inventory (accessed August 2010).

Center for Non-violent Communication (2005b) *Needs inventory,* online, www.cnvc.org/en/Training/needs-inventory (accessed August 2010).

Craig G 'The writing on our walls', *The Palace of Possibilities,* 1 (2), online, www.eftuniverse.com (accessed October 2010)

Faupel A, Herrick E & Sharp P (1998) *Anger Management: A Practical Guide,* David Fulton Publishers Ltd, London.

Ginott HG (1975) *Teacher and Child,* Conguent Communications, New York.

Ginott HG (2003) *Between Parent and Child,* Three Rivers Press*, New York.*

Johnson RA (2008) *Inner Gold: Understanding Psychological Projection,* Koa Books, Hawaii.

Karpman S (1968) 'Fairy tales and script drama analysis', *Transactional Analysis Bulletin,* 7 (26), pp39–43.

Lilley R (2002) *Dealing with Difficult People,* Kogan Page, London.

Meade M (1993) 'The second layer: anger, hatred, outrage', Bly R, Hillman J and Meades M (eds) *The Rag and Bone Shop of the Heart: Poems for Men,* Harper Perennial, London.

Rosenberg MB (2000) *Raising Children Compassionately,* Center for Non-violent Communication, La Crescenta, CA.

Rosenberg MB (1999) *Non-violent Communication: A Language of Compassion,* PuddleDancer Press, Del Mar, CA.

Whitehouse E & Pudney W (1996) *A Volcano in My Tummy: Helping Children to Handle Anger,* New Society Publishers, Cabriola Island, BC, Canada.